Rabbi Shmuel Herzfeld

Renewal

Inspirational Lessons of Rosh Hashanah

The Orlofsky Edition

Copyright © Shmuel Herzfeld
Jerusalem 2015/5775

All rights reserved. No part of this publication may be translated, reproduced, stored in a retrieval system or transmitted, in any form or by any means, electronic, mechanical, photocopying, recording or otherwise, without express written permission from the publishers.

Cover Design: Talya Shachar-Albocher
Typesetting: Irit Nachum

ISBN: 978-965-229-806-5

1 3 5 7 9 8 6 4 2

Gefen Publishing House Ltd.	Gefen Books
6 Hatzvi Street	11 Edison Place
Jerusalem 94386, Israel	Springfield, NJ 07081
972-2-538-0247	516-593-1234
orders@gefenpublishing.com	orders@gefenpublishing.com

www.gefenpublishing.com

Printed in Israel   *Send for our free catalog*

Library of Congress Cataloging-in-Publication Data

Herzfeld, Shmuel, author.
Renewal : inspirational lessons for Rosh Hashanah / by Rabbi Shmuel Herzfeld. — Orlofsky edition.
   pages cm
ISBN 978-965-229-806-5
1. Rosh ha-Shanah sermons.   2. Jewish sermons, English. I. Title.
BM747.R6H47 2015
296.4'7315—dc23
                    2015011764

Dedicated to Ohev Sholom - The National Synagogue.
A shul that never stopped believing in the possibility of renewal.

Dedicated on the occasion of the bar mitzvah of our son
Elitzur Simcha Nachum Gitler

And in honor of his grandfathers
Henry Koschitzky
David Gitler

May you always be searching out new and wondrous ways of loving Hashem and living life to its fullest potential and thereby fulfill the words of the prophet, "Turn us to You, Hashem, and we shall return. Renew our days of old" (Eikhah 5:21).

Joseph and Leelah Gitler

מוקדש לרגל חגיגת בר המצווה של בננו

אליצור שמחה נחום גיטלר

ולכבוד שני סביו

חיים בן ישראל (הנרי) קושיצקי

דוד בן יעקב יוסף גיטלר

יהי רצון שתשאף תמיד לדרכים חדשות ומיוחדות
לאהוב את הבורא,
ולחיות את חייך באופן מלא,
ויתקיימו בך דברי הנביא,
"השיבנו ה' אליך ונשובה, חדש ימינו כקדם" (איכה ה:כא).

יעקב יוסף ולילך גיטלר

Dedicated to my friend and mentor Steve Schram.

The rabbis teach us:

"Make for yourself a mentor and acquire for yourself a friend" (Avot 1:6).

This book is dedicated to the theme of renewal, and knowing you has meant a renewal of my life. I am forever grateful for your incredible friendship and mentoring which have been a source of strength to me in both my business and my personal life. You are a truly righteous man, who is always there for me and so many others.

Thank you for your love, patience, and guidance.

Love,
Aaron Orlofsky

In memory of our dear friend
Henry Mitrani, *a"h*

who taught us to appreciate each day to the fullest, whose bright smile inspired us all, and whose love of family is a shining example for our community.

We extend our love and condolences to the Mitrani family, in whom his memory lives on most strongly:

Rose Mitrani

Mandi and David Lowenstein

Jaclyn and Gadi Rozmaryn

Shana, Elie, Liat, Kira, Itai, and Maya

Aaron, Ahuva, Avigail, Elana, and Izzy Orlofsky

Other books by this author

Fifty-Four Pick Up, 2012

Food for the Spirit: *Inspirational Lessons from the Yom Kippur Service* (the Orlofsky edition), 2014

The Lieberman Open Orthodox Haggadah
(the Orlofsky edition), 2015

Contents

Acknowledgments		xi
Introduction		1
Chapter 1	Is a Return Always an Option?	3
Chapter 2	Three Lessons of Rosh Hashanah	8
Chapter 3	The Avimelekh Syndrome	15
Chapter 4	God Will Gather Me In	20
Chapter 5	Basic Nourishment	25
Chapter 6	Can You Hear Me Now?	31
Chapter 7	The Story of Chanah: From Loneliness to Community	37
Chapter 8	Mirror Image	43
Chapter 9	A Reinvigorated Evangelical Jew	49
Chapter 10	The Obligations of Man and the Mercy of God	56
Chapter 11	Climbing the Mountain Path	62
Chapter 12	Crowning the King	69
Chapter 13	How to Keep a New Year's Resolution	75
Chapter 14	Rekindling Our Romance with God	82

Chapter 15	Striving for Spiritual Honesty	90
Chapter 16	Working toward a Communal Prayer	98
Chapter 17	The Sounds of the Shofar against the Backdrop of War	101
Chapter 18	A Modern-Day Meaning to the Akeidah	106
Chapter 19	Pray with Power	110
Chapter 20	True, Honest Jews	116
Chapter 21	Let Us Listen	120

Acknowledgments

The publication of this book would not have been possible without the very generous support of two families: Joseph and Leelah Gitler and Aaron and Ahuva Orlofsky.

Joseph and Leelah Gitler are role models to the world. They dedicate their entire lives to helping other people. It is a blessing that this book is being sponsored in honor of their son Elitzur's bar mitzvah. I remember very well the day when Elitzur was born and it has been a real treat to watch him grow up. I bless Elitzur on the occasion of his bar mitzvah that he walk in the footsteps of his incredible parents and amazing grandparents and dedicate his life to the service of others in the way that his parents and grandparents have chosen to do.

Aaron and Ahuva have given our congregation and family so much support over the years that I cannot adequately express the gratitude that I feel toward them. Their constant support gives me the encouragement and inspiration necessary to be a congregational rabbi. A congregational rabbi is often expected to inspire others. But I can only attempt to inspire others if I myself am inspired, and it is people like Aaron and Ahuva who inspire me and enable me to be a better rabbi.

It is a tremendous honor for me to have my name associated with these two families.

This project started with the hard work of my dear friend and Daf Yomi partner Baruch Roth. Baruch spent many hours going through all my divrei Torah and collecting the ones that relate to the holiday of Rosh Hashanah. He then edited them slightly and passed them along to me. His dedication to this project was essential. It is especially sweet for me that while working on this project together, Baruch and I were also able to study and complete tractate Rosh Hashanah as part of the Daf Yomi cycle.

I am deeply grateful to the entire Ohev Sholom – The National Synagogue congregation for their support in all of the projects and divrei Torah that I undertake. I thank them for listening to these divrei Torah and offering me helpful and constructive feedback so that we can grow together.

I am thankful to my rebbe, Rabbi Avi Weiss, who would often spend time with me working through these divrei Torah so I had a clearer message to communicate.

I thank the whole team at Gefen for their amazing and professional help. I am especially grateful to Tziporah Levine for her editing skills. It is an honor to work with my publisher, Ilan Greenfield, who has extended himself above and beyond the limit of what mere professional responsibility requires.

Above all, I thank Rhanni, my wife, without whom none of what I am able to accomplish would be possible. I thank our children, Lea, Roey, Elai, Max, Shia, Kolbi, and Bear for helping me love and appreciate the holiday of Rosh Hashanah.

Introduction

In August 2004, I had the great privilege and honor of being appointed as the rabbi of what was then called Ohev Sholom Talmud Torah, and which subsequently became Ohev Sholom – The National Synagogue.

The congregation then was on wobbly legs. The first Shabbat I spent with the synagogue there was barely a minyan – twelve men to be precise. This was a disconcerting fact since the synagogue had once numbered more than eight hundred families strong and the synagogue building contained a majestic main sanctuary that held more than 750 seats. There was also a smaller chapel in the building that held 110 seats.

The first few weeks that I was in the synagogue we held all of our services in the smaller chapel in order to achieve a greater intimacy in our service. But as Rosh Hashanah approached I wasn't sure where we should pray. We were expecting no more than a few dozen people for the High Holidays and the chapel could easily hold this number. On the other hand, there was something about the majestic sanctuary that was calling to me, and indeed to others in the congregation as well. One of the long-time members of the synagogue, a man named Sid, asked to meet with me on the eve of Rosh Hashanah. He begged me to hold the services in the large sanctuary since he felt that that would be a sign that his beloved congregation had turned the corner and was entering a period of growth.

Indeed, we did worship in the large sanctuary that Rosh Hashanah and every Rosh Hashanah since then. I explained to the congregation that there are two main themes to the holiday of Rosh Hashanah: judgment and renewal.

Many people focus on the theme of Rosh Hashanah as a day of judgment, but no less significant is that it is a day of renewal. By praying in the main sanctuary we were declaring that we were yearning for a renewal, a rebirth of our synagogue, and a return to our golden years. Our prayers in this respect were answered and our congregation did undergo a renaissance, which I consider myself very fortunate to be a part of.

The theme of renewal tells us that we have an opportunity to start over and change the trajectory of our lives. In order to do this we first need to be honest with ourselves about our shortcomings and our goals. This is where judgment comes in. If we submit ourselves to the judgment of God then we will have a chance to renew our lives for the better.

These two themes – judgment and renewal – are the themes of the divrei Torah in this book. But they are really one intertwined theme, as the ultimate goal of Rosh Hashanah is to inspire us to achieve a renewal.

Rosh Hashanah is an exhilarating holiday. I eagerly anticipate its arrival from the moment we first blast the shofar at the beginning of Elul and I miss it dearly when the holiday ends.

It is an honor to share with you why I love so much this holiday of renewal.

Chapter 1
Is a Return Always an Option?

On Rosh Hashanah, drama fills the air. We feel the tension of the courtroom as we await our judgment. We feel the tension of the liturgy as we read about life's fragility in prayers like u'Netaneh Tokef. And we feel the tension of the shofar blowing, as we all nervously wait to make sure that a pure sound comes from the shofar.

With all this tension, there is one emotional reaction that keeps recurring: crying. On the first day of Rosh Hashanah, we read in the Torah of how Hagar and Yishmael both cry after they are exiled from the house of Avraham and Sarah. In the haftarah of the first day we read about the cries of Chanah, as she was a barren woman. In the haftarah of the second day we read the verse, "*Rachel mevakah al banehah*" (Rachel cries for her children). On the second day we also read the story of the Akeidah, the near sacrifice of Yitzchak, and here the Midrash teaches that both Sarah and an angel cried.

Maybe the most poignant cries that we hear on Rosh Hashanah are the sounds of the shofar. According to the Talmud in tractate *Rosh Hashanah*, the *teruah* sound that the shofar makes is supposed to mimic the cries of the mother of Sisera, the ancient, defeated general. The sounds that we constantly hear on Rosh Hashanah are the sounds of crying.

Why is everyone crying? Why does crying dominate our day of judgment?

The reason for these cries is tightly connected to the concept of *teshuvah*, repentance, which is a central aspect of our *Yamim Noraim*, our Days of Awe.

In order to understand the concept of *teshuvah*, we should focus on one particularly difficult passage in the Torah, which at first glance might seem entirely unconnected to Rosh Hashanah.

Says God to Moshe: I'll take you out of Egypt using great miracles and signs. And I guarantee that Paroh will not send you out before I punish him with the ten plagues. The reason is: "*va'ani aksheh et lev Paroh*" (I shall harden the heart of Paroh; Shemot 7:2). God is telling Moshe that He will not allow Paroh to repent.

This is an extremely difficult idea. How is it possible that Paroh is denied this ability to repent? After all, *teshuvah* is a central tenet of Judaism. It's not only central to Judaism, it's also central to the world. It allows people to realize that they are not always identified with their past mistakes. It gives hope to us all. To take away the concept of *teshuvah* from someone is to strip this person – and, indeed, all of us – of positive energy and optimism. How is it possible that the Torah can say that Paroh did not have the ability to repent?

Rambam (Maimonides) writes: "It is possible that someone can commit such a great sin or sins that the right to repent is removed from that person and that person has no ability to abandon the wickedness" (*Mishneh Torah, Hilkhot Teshuvah* 6:3). This is how Rambam explains the hardening of Paroh's heart. Paroh had committed so many sins in his life that he reached the point of no return. He simply could not turn back the clock anymore and erase what had happened. Nothing Paroh could do could ever change the fact that he had acted so harshly toward the Jewish people. And because he had acted this way for a significant amount of time, he actually lost the ability to repent.

Rambam is teaching us that the right to repent is not absolute! It is a privilege, and it doesn't always work. But why doesn't it work? Shouldn't we all have the right to turn back the clock and ask God for forgiveness? According to Rambam, the answer is – no. Paroh's punishment is his tragic loss of the right to do *teshuvah*. He lost the ability to control his own life. The hardening of his heart was simply the result of his acting too wickedly for too long a time. He had reached a point from which he could no longer fully come back.

Nechama Leibowitz (*Iyunim Chadashim b'Sefer Shemot* [Jerusalem, 1973], 116) explains that the situation is similar to a person struggling with an addiction, in that our own repetitive behavior makes it harder for us to repent. In her commentary she compares Paroh to the literary character Macbeth, who says, "Things bad begun make strong themselves by ill" (*Macbeth*, act 3, scene 2). The first time someone commits a sin, the action is a free one, and the person has total control. But once addicted to that sin, the person loses the ability to control his life.

In this sense an addict is similar to a person who has the lost the right to repent. The Mishnah teaches us, "*Aveirah goreret aveirah*" (One sin leads to another; *Avot* 4:2). Sometimes we choose a path in life and the path seems irreversible. The great fear is that a bad path will truly become irreversible. We must always act before we reach the point of no return.

The reality is that there are many actions that we do in life that simply can't be reversed. If someone wastes away his body on drugs or alcohol, he will feel the physical effects. Even if he is regretful of the fact that he took drugs, the unfortunate truth is that his body has been physically weakened. Similarly, if someone made a mistake and was convicted of a crime, that crime will forever be with him. Regardless of how much he regrets and repents, that crime will always be a part of his existence.

This is one aspect of *teshuvah*. It is not the most pleasant thought in the world. And in some ways it is a devastating realization. Maybe this is why everyone is crying on Rosh Hashanah. Rosh Hashanah is a time to take stock of ourselves. And often when we look closely we see that we've made mistakes. Sometimes we've made really big mistakes that we just can't change.

This is one aspect of *teshuvah* – looking back at the mistakes of the past and realizing that we messed up. When we look back at those mistakes, we sometimes cry. That is the sound of the shofar's *teruah*. It is the sound of our cries for our past mistakes.

The sound of the *teruah* should cause us to realize that not all of our mistakes can be corrected. Sometimes we make a decision, and we have to live with the consequences of our decision for the rest of our life. The cries of the *teruah* urgently remind us: Don't let our lives get to that point of no return. Correct our mistakes, while we still can.

The shofar also has another sound: a *tekiah*, a single long blast. This sound points to another aspect of *teshuvah*. If Heaven forbid, tragically, our lives have reached that point and we have made mistakes that can't be corrected – we've committed horrible sins that simply can't be erased. What then should we do?

If the *teruah* represents our cries, then the *tekiah*, the single note going on and on, represents our unlimited human potential. This is the other aspect of *teshuvah* that must always accompany our cries. We must realize that sometimes learning from our mistakes can enable us to realize our potential. Some of our mistakes can never escape us, but that doesn't mean we shouldn't still strive to accomplish great things in this world.

I'll always have with me the image of Mickey Mantle as a dying man. He was one of the greatest baseball players ever, but toward the end of his life he was a shell of himself. This great physical specimen cut his life short by many years because he drank far too much alcohol. Try as he could, once he was sick he could not undo his weakened state nor the thousands of times that he had drunk to excess. But as a dying man he strove toward a very important goal: in a very public manner, he told people not to repeat his mistakes. Even though he was dying as a result of his mistakes, he still strove to fulfill his destiny as a leader in this world ("Time in a Bottle," *Sports Illustrated*, April 18, 1994).

The blast of the *tekiah* contrasts with the cries of the *teruah*. It reminds us that even though our errors might be great, we can sometimes use the experience of our sins as a means to help others in the world. A former addict, who may never be able to fully recover his health and on a personal level may forever be scarred, can help the world by lecturing about the dangers of drugs. Or someone who made many mistakes in his personal life decisions can use the mistakes he made as a way of educating others and helping other people avoid family tragedies.

This is the message of the shofar and the message of *teshuvah*. Realize that we can make mistakes in our lives that are irreversible. One aspect of *teshuvah* is to cry over those mistakes and to try to stop ourselves from reaching that nadir of no return. The *teruah* with its sad cries encapsulates that message. But those cries must always be accompanied by the *tekiah*, the single blast which symbolizes our hope and potential. The *tekiah* points to the other aspect of *teshuvah*: the realization that we can use the lessons learned from our mistakes as a means of fulfilling our destinies.

People who made monumental mistakes in their lives still have a path to redemption. They might not be able to change their past and their sins might never be erased, but what they can do is to work hard to bring light to the world. If through one's life experience one is able to prevent others from getting the hard heart of Paroh then one is truly fulfilling the spirit of a return to God. One who does that is living the ultimate renewal of one's life.

Chapter 2
Three Lessons of Rosh Hashanah

In August 2005, Hurricane Katrina arrived and devastated the city of New Orleans and many surrounding areas. It was one of the worst storms in American history. Many people died and many lives were devastated. Since it happened right before Rosh Hashanah, it was on everyone's minds as they recited their prayers that year. As we sang the words of the liturgy, "Who [will die] by water?" we all thought of the people whose lives had been devastated by the Katrina tragedy.

When we see such darkness and horrific devastation we should look to Rosh Hashanah for guidance and to be our light through the most difficult times. In the days leading up to Rosh Hashanah we declare in our Selichot prayers: *"Lekha, Hashem, hatzedakah"* (For You, Hashem, is righteousness). How should we understand that phrase when we see such seemingly random devastation?

One of the messages of Rosh Hashanah is that we recognize God as King even though we don't understand all of His ways.

What does it mean to say God is King? It means that we are not king! That is a fundamental lesson of Rosh Hashanah – We are not kings, and we should not view ourselves as kings. This is the lesson of humility.

Rosh Hashanah is filled with laws and prayers reminding us of this powerful lesson. The emphasis of the day is on God's Kingship. The fragility of our lives reminds us that we come from dust and to dust we shall return. We dare to think that we are worthy of praise or greatness. Well, on Rosh Hashanah we look back at our sins of the past year and we remember how often we sinned. How dare we imagine ourselves to be great, when we are filled with so much sin! Indeed, the very symbol of Rosh Hashanah is not merely a shofar, but specifically a *bent* shofar – a reminder that we must approach God with a humble heart.

Rabbi Moshe Chayyim Luzzatto, the author of *Mesillat Yesharim* (*The Path of the Just*), teaches us that lack of humility is the origin of all sin (chapters 22–23). Only one who feels arrogant can be bold enough to sin. What does it mean to be humble? How do we achieve this state of humility?

Mesillat Yesharim explains that humility consists in a person realizing that he does not deserve praise and honor both because of his natural limitations as well as because of his accumulated sins. True humility is the recognition that all of our good qualities are simply designations from God. They do not make us greater or lesser individuals. If one is smart, athletic, strong, or creative it is simply like having brown hair or blond hair. It is a designation by God, not a reflection of one's greatness.

According to *Mesillat Yesharim*, the characteristic that we must be most on guard against, the factor that most likely will lead us to sin is superior intelligence. One who is blessed by God with intelligence will often feel self-important and better than others. This is a great sin, tantamount to idolatry. For, indeed, no one is so smart that there is no one else smarter. No one is so smart as to not make mistakes. And no one is so smart as to understand the ways of God. Yet we sin by thinking that our intelligence makes us better than others. This leads us to pride and away from humility. And, when we act with pride, we are following our own desires and not the path of God.

We in the twenty-first century like to think we are gaining more and more control over God. We are living this great sin of superior intelligence. We have made phenomenal technological advances, we've discovered new ways to fight disease – yet Rosh Hashanah reminds us that only God is King of the universe. Our intelligence and our abilities are woefully inadequate before the great mysteries of the world.

One summer I lost my voice for three months and subsequently I had to undergo two surgeries to fix my vocal chords. One of the things that I realized was how desperately frail our bodies really are and how so much of what I do professionally is dependent upon being able to speak and project myself clearly. I know it's a little shallow to talk about losing a voice as a sign of a frail body. My personal inconvenience can't be compared to the very real physical pain that many have gone through. But for me losing my voice hit home; it enabled me to see my own humanity a little bit more clearly. Losing my voice showed me how powerless I was to control my own fate. It helped me internalize *Mesillat Yesharim*'s understanding of humility – a humility that is a recognition of our insignificance and imperfection before God's awesomeness, majesty, and beauty.

One time I took my car to my mechanic in the heart of the winter. I told him, "The heat is not working. I'm freezing." The mechanic told me, "That's good, Rabbi. It teaches you humility." He was right. A cold car does teach humility. I think about that lesson often, but not nearly often enough.

If we need a reminder, we need merely look at devastating tragedies like Hurricane Katrina, and after that Hurricane Sandy.

No one can justifiably claim to understand the ways of God, but we can look at events like Katrina and Sandy and remind ourselves that we are not masters of the universe; we are powerless before God's world.

This is the first lesson of Rosh Hashanah. We are not kings; instead, we must be loyal servants. Or as Rabbi Jack Riemer told me, "The Jewish religion can be summarized in two sentences: there is a God in the world – and it is not me."

Let me now share with you another lesson of Rosh Hashanah; it is a second understanding of humility. On the second day of Rosh Hashanah we read the story of the Akeidah. God tells Avraham to sacrifice his beloved firstborn son, Yitzchak. Let's leave aside the enormous ethical and theological problems this act presents. Emotionally, as a father, the Akeidah boggles my mind. I look at my children and I love them more than anything in the world; the thought of such an act makes me shudder.

And that is exactly the point. True humility is the recognition that everything and anything that we have does not belong to us. True humility is the belief that nothing in our lives is more important than our relationship with God.

Rabbi Joseph Soloveitchik once explained this very Torah passage to a priest. He wrote:

> Children are the greatest and most precious charge God has entrusted to man's custody…. Man, willy-nilly, must acknowledge this irrevocable though bitter truth; he must be ready to lose everything, if losing is what God demands. He must always answer the call summoning him to perform heroically the movement of withdrawal from the most tightly knit and natural community on earth – that of father and son….
>
> The offering of Isaac is exemplary of this type of sacrificial service of God…. He wanted Abraham to abandon all pretense of possessiveness, all claims of

unity and identity, all hopes of self-perpetuation and immortalization through Isaac and return him to Whom he belongs. (Rabbi Joseph B. Soloveitchik, *Community, Covenant and Commitment: Selected Letters and Communications*, ed. Nathaniel Helfgot [Ktav, 2005], 300)

This is the second type of humility. It is the recognition that nothing we have really belongs to us. It is a humility that declares that nothing we own, possess, or hold dear is more valuable than our relationship with God. It is the humility of all our earthly relationships.

In a very sad way, we all learn this lesson when we witness horrific natural disasters. Often the victims themselves internalize this lesson and understand it better than anyone else. Torn from their loved ones, they will often turn to God in recognition of the concept that the only relationship that can never be terminated is a relationship with God. The most spiritual ones will recognize that the tragedy they have experienced will give them a greater relationship with God than many of us can ever comprehend. They will be able to internalize the lessons of humility for the rest of their lives.

The rest of us can gain insight into humility by following the teachings of the Torah and the words of our prayers. The Torah's teachings remind us that our lives must follow rules that are not of our own making. Some rules we understand and some we don't, but it must always be clear to us that we don't make the rules; we must submit to God. The words of our prayers said throughout the day are a reminder that it is God Who is King and not us. As we bow down in our prayers, we remind ourselves that our relationship with God is supreme.

This brings us to a third lesson. The reason it is so important to live these lessons of humility is because humility is a prerequisite for godliness. The Talmud in *Rosh Hashanah* (32a) states that we recite ten verses in each of the three additional parts of Musaf because the world was created through ten utterances. Rosh Hashanah celebrates creation. We praise God for the creation of the world and we remind ourselves that we must create acts of goodness – godly acts – in this world. When we recite these verses we are reminding ourselves that we need to be creative in this world.

Acting godlike – being generous, good, charitable, kind, forgiving – is our role in this world. Such acts can make us feel great; they can make us feel like we are God. In order for our good acts to be God-serving, rather than only self-serving, they must come from a place of humility – otherwise our actions are akin to idolatry.

When a tragedy arises from a natural disaster it is often devastating and many of us are left feeling numb. But what we often see in response to such tragedies are some of the most uplifting and inspiring expressions of humanity.

After Katrina, for example, I saw many volunteers and caregivers acting with great dignity and without any fanfare. People like Rabbi Sol Strassberg, a rabbi in Nashville, Tennessee, who drove an 18-wheeler down to Mississippi, or Rabbi Barry Gellman, a rabbi in Houston, who woke up early in the morning to serve breakfast to Katrina victims stranded in the Houston Astrodome. And after Hurricane Sandy, my friend Aaron arranged on his own for a truck to bring generators to homes in Long Island that were without electricity.

These are three fundamental lessons of Rosh Hashanah. Firstly, have humility and recognize that we are not in complete control of this world. Secondly, be humble and recognize that our relationship with God is the only relationship that will never be terminated. And thirdly, when we perform acts of goodness we should perform them with humility. Give charity with humility. Volunteer with humility. Teach Torah with humility.

Shai Agnon tells the following story.

> One year as the congregation was waiting to recite the Selichot prayers on the Saturday night prior to Rosh Hashanah they were delayed because the great rabbi of the town, Rabbi Avraham of Tresk, was still sitting in his home studying Torah. Finally, one of his grandchildren came and asked him, "The time has come to recite Selichot. Why are you not going to daven in the *beit midrash*?" The tzaddik answered, "I am certainly not ready. How can I go to recite Selichot? The Selichot begin with the words, '*Lekha, Hashem, hatzedakah*' (For You, Hashem, is righteousness), and I know the matter is not so. Indeed, in the custom of the world, what does a father do to a son who, God forbid, misbehaves? He nevertheless is good to him, so that he doesn't do more bad things. How much more so, in our case, where we are righteous and good, and God can have no complaints against us." After he said this, the tzaddik was silent for a while before continuing, "But then we say, '*v'lanu boshet hapanim*' (but we are shamefaced). This is the truth. Thus, let us go to recite Selichot." (Shai Agnon, *Yamim Noraim* [Hebrew; 1979], 45)

When we see tragedy we sometimes cry out, "*Lekha, Hashem, hatzedakah?*" – Are you righteous, God? But the lesson of Rosh Hashanah is that even though we have no answer to this, we must continue, "*v'lanu boshet hapanim*" – we must always respond with humility.

Chapter 3
The Avimelekh Syndrome

Every year we celebrate Rosh Hashanah and we accept resolutions upon ourselves. But how many of us really change? How many of us stop our bad habits forever? How many of us really renew ourselves on Rosh Hashanah?

When people think about Rosh Hashanah, they think about the shofar, or the beautiful Musaf; perhaps they think about the Akeidah story, or the prayer of Chanah, or even God's promise to Sarah that Yitzchak will be born. But there is another major character of Rosh Hashanah who we often forget about.

That character is Avimelekh. We read about Avimelekh in the Torah reading of the first day of Rosh Hashanah (Bereishit 21). Of all people, he is uniquely suited to teach the secret of change. Avimelekh's story is included because it carries with it three central messages of Rosh Hashanah. Two of the messages teach us the key to changing our behavior and the third message teaches us about God's behavior.

In the Torah reading, God promises Sarah and Avraham that they will have a child named Yitzchak. Sarah initially laughs and questions God, but then Yitzchak is born. Following that Hagar and Yishmael are sent away by Avraham. Hagar despairs that she and Yishmael will die, but then God promises that He will make Yishmael into a great nation. They are saved and Yishmael is raised in the desert.

The Torah reading could have very easily ended there – but it doesn't. A powerful Philistine man named Avimelekh appears on the scene. Avimelekh approaches Avraham to make a treaty with him.

This is not the first time we've met with Avimelekh. In just the previous chapter, the Torah relates that Avraham came to Gerar. Avraham was concerned that Avimelekh, the king of Gerar, would kill him and marry his wife Sarah. So Avraham passes off Sarah as his sister. Immediately Avimelekh sends his men and kidnaps Sarah. When God threatens to destroy Avimelekh, Avimelekh responds with what sounds like two good excuses. He says, "He told me, 'She is my sister.'" It is Avraham's fault. And it is also Sarah's fault: "And she also told me, 'He is my brother.'" Avimelekh essentially claims: "It is not my fault. I am innocent."

Avimelekh's excuses here may sound credible, but once we read about Avimelekh's second encounter with Avraham we begin to wonder. In this second encounter, which concludes the Rosh Hashanah Torah reading, Avimelekh approaches Avraham and says, "I noticed that God has been with you. Let's make a treaty." Avraham agrees to this, but then the very next verse tells us that "Avraham rebuked Avimelekh on account of the wells that Avimelekh's servants had stolen."

In other words, they made a treaty and right away Avraham's wells were stolen. Here is how Avimelekh responds: "I don't know *who* did this! *You* never told me. And I *never* heard about it before today." Three different times Avimelekh denies responsibility. He passes the buck and says it is not his fault. But now we know that Avimelekh is already the master of excuses. Now we can see that his excuses are lame and weak.

A fundamental lesson of Rosh Hashanah is for us to stop making excuses. As my teacher, Rabbi Saul Berman, explains, the story of Avimelekh is read on Rosh Hashanah because it teaches us how *not* to act. The essence of the Days of Awe is that we must acknowledge all of the errors that we made in the previous year. We cannot come closer to God unless we admit that we erred – we have sinned, we were at fault.

We live in a society that loves to make excuses. *It wasn't my fault. There were mitigating circumstances.* This is the Avimelekh syndrome. When we judge others we must be sensitive to any possible excuse and not judge harshly, but when we judge ourselves we must look a little more closely. We must not fall prone to the Avimelekh syndrome.

If we want to come close to God, if we want to make real change in our lives, then we must not make excuses for our behavior. We should acknowledge our errors and work on fixing them. This is the first step of *teshuvah*: acknowledging our errors.

Take a moment and think. What errors have you made over the last year – big or small?

*****

Avimelekh also teaches us a second lesson about *teshuvah*. Again it is a lesson in how *not* to act.

Avimelekh approached Avraham and requested a treaty not only for himself but also for future generations. Avraham agrees and Avimelekh recognizes that Avraham dug the wells at Beer Sheva. And there the matter was settled; they had a treaty after all. The treaty should have lasted for a few generations.

Yet, lo and behold, years later Yitzchak again gets into a dispute with Avimelekh. After Avraham died Avimelekh's henchmen closed up Avraham's wells (Bereishit 26:18). So much for his promises to Avraham!

Avimelekh teaches us how *not* to act. Avimelekh doesn't keep his word; he makes promises and treaties and they are just words. We cannot catch the Avimelekh syndrome. We must each begin Rosh Hashanah by making a promise and we must work on ourselves to keep our promises.

Pick one thing and commit to it. Promise yourself. You might want to verbalize it softly, just like you verbalize your Amidah.

*****

And now we come to the third lesson of the Avimelekh story. This lesson teaches us about God's behavior.

What is the connection between the Avimelekh story and the first half of the Torah reading? The Torah reading begins by telling us, *"Hashem pakad et Sarah"* (God remembered Sarah). Sarah had given up hope; she had given up on life. When the angels came to tell her she was having a baby, she thought God was laughing at her. Can you imagine anything sadder than thinking that God is laughing at you? She thought God had forgotten about her, but in the end she learned that God remembered her. He had never forgotten her.

In Sarah's case she was blessed with a child, which was something she and Avraham had been yearning for. But the message of the story is not that Hashem will always give us whatever we ask for. Rather, the message is that our relationship with God is eternal. If we fully commit to Hashem then we will gain enormous spiritual strength from that relationship and it will be a source of empowerment for us throughout our lives.

People forget. People break their promises, but God will always be there for us to hold our hand. God has a covenant with us – a relationship with us that will always strengthen our lives.

That is the third lesson of the Avimelekh story. We must do our part, we must acknowledge our errors and keep our resolutions, but the end result is that God will remember us. The Avimelekh's of the world won't remember us, but Hashem always will.

Even when we think God is laughing at us, maybe He is really remembering us.

Reading the story of Avimelekh on Rosh Hashanah reminds us not to end up like him – not to make excuses for ourselves and not to break our promises. If we do our part, then in the end God will remember us. God will guard us and protect us. God's presence in our lives will always be there to enrich and nourish.

Chapter 4
God Will Gather Me In

One year I noticed a sign on the street advertising that Bob Dylan would be performing in concert in DC right around Sukkot time. Of course, I sent him an invitation to join us for a meal in our Sukkah.

Bob Dylan was born as Robert Zimmerman, a nice Jewish boy from Minnesota. He led the life of a rock star. He was a hit musician, a brilliant poet, and an inspiration to many people. He was an activist and a symbol. He also had a life of ups and downs. He went through multiple relationships and periods of depression and despair. At one point he broke his neck falling off a motorcycle and had to fight his way back to life.

Spiritually, he also wandered from his roots. For a while he embraced all religions. Then, in the late 1970s, he became a born-again Christian and produced albums celebrating his faith in Christianity. But can anyone ever really leave their roots? In the late '80s Dylan seemed to reconnect to his *Yiddishkeit*. And based upon the fact that multiple media reports have placed him in a synagogue at different points over the past few years he seems to have remained with it ever since.

Here is my favorite Bob Dylan story. On February 20, 1991, Bob Dylan was given a Grammy award for lifetime achievement. After accepting his trophy, Dylan said:

> "Well, my daddy, he didn't leave me much, you know he was a very simple man, but what he did tell me was this, he did say, 'Son,' he said" – there was a long pause, nervous laughter from the crowd – "'you know it's possible to become so defiled in this world that your own father and mother will abandon you and if that happens, God will always believe in your ability to mend your ways.'"
>
> …Dylan's remarks were almost a verbatim account of the commentary of Rabbi Shimshon Rafael Hirsch…: "Even if I were so depraved that my own mother and father would abandon me to my own devices, God would still gather me up and believe in my ability to mend my ways." (Taken from http://www.radiohazak.com/Dylgramm.html)

Rav Hirsch was a brilliant rabbi in Germany in the nineteenth century. His comments (which presumably inspired Dylan) were written for the words of psalm 27, which we recite every day in the month of Elul leading up to Rosh Hashanah, "For though my father and mother forsake me, God will gather me in."

This psalm was written by King David to express his loneliness. King David was the most powerful man of his generation. He was a great warrior. He ruled all of Israel and conquered Jerusalem. No one had been able to do that before. He had six wives and many children.

And yet, David was a profoundly lonely man. He was racked

with the guilt of the sins he had committed and with despair over the losses he had suffered. His first son from Batsheva died as an infant. Then another one of his sons, Amnon, assaulted his own sister, Tamar. David's other son, Avshalom, then killed Amnon and led a rebellion against David. David felt betrayed by everyone around him. Upon hearing of Avshalom's death he cries out in pain, "Avshalom, Avshalom, my son."

David put this feeling of loneliness to paper and he wrote a beautiful psalm which is the center of our liturgy. In the psalm he expresses both his loneliness and his reliance upon God. He cries, "For though my father and mother forsake me, God will gather me in." No matter what he has done, he feels that God will still embrace him and draw him in closer. Even if his own parents give up on him, God still makes room for him.

The Torah contains the story of another spiritual giant who might have also felt David's sense of loneliness and betrayal. The Torah reading for the second day of Rosh Hashanah tells the story of the Akeidah. Avraham leads Yitzchak up Mount Moriah and binds him on the altar.

When we analyze this story we often ask ourselves: How could Avraham have done this? How could he have had the strength to tie his own son up with the intention of slaughtering him? But let us for a moment think about it from Yitzchak's perspective. Imagine how Yitzchak must have felt as his own father – his only father, the one whom he loved – bound him and stood above him with a knife, intending to slaughter him.

Even scarier than the knife which stopped just inches from his throat must have been the sense of abandonment. Can you imagine? Your own father abandoning you!

Yitzchak's feelings of abandonment at that moment were infinitely deeper than any that we are likely to experience. Yet on some level, we can all relate to being abandoned. We have all been abandoned at one point in our lives. And we will all be abandoned. Our loved ones have died and will die; our friends have forgotten us and will forget us; our bosses or customers don't appreciate us. We can get very lonely.

At that moment Yitzchak might have thought: *"Ki avi v'imi azavuni, va'Hashem yaasfeni"* (For though my father and mother forsake me, God will gather me in).

We too cry out: *"Ki avi v'imi azavuni, va'Hashem yaasfeni."*

Even though everyone around us will abandon us, God will still draw us in. We can return to God for a relationship. On Rosh Hashanah we are reminded that as long as we are with Hashem we are never alone. Hashem will be there to comfort us and be our friend. No matter how dark life gets, Hashem is by our side.

Isn't this what the sound of the shofar is really all about? We often forget to focus on the original meaning of the shofar blast. The Torah tells us to blow a *tekiah* to "gather the congregation" (Bamidbar 10:7). The basic – perhaps the primary – purpose of the shofar is to gather us in. At its core, the shofar is a cry from Hashem calling us to Him; He calls to us and tells us to come home to His embrace.

In that same passage in the Torah, a secondary meaning of the shofar also appears. The Torah states, "You must blast a *teruah* and then you will travel" (verse 5). After the *tekiah* was used to gather the people, the *teruah* was then used to signal the start of the travels of the Israelites in the desert. On a symbolic level we can understand this to mean that if we allow Hashem to gather us in we can then travel with Him. We can journey with God, holding His hand, and ascend to higher places. Once we allow Hashem to gather us in then we can travel with Hashem.

One of the most beautiful verses from the Rosh Hashanah Musaf is taken from Yirmiyahu: *"Zakharti lakh chesed ne'urayikh… lekhtekh acharai ba'midbar"* (I remember the kindness of your youth…how you followed Me through the wilderness; Yirmiyahu 2:2). Yirmiyahu is telling us that God remembers us how we once were – pure and innocent and like children. He gathers us up and believes in us when no one else does. God is like a parent, always believing in us.

On Rosh Hashanah we remind ourselves that God is King of the universe. Since God is King, who are we? We are of course princes, nobles with an awesome opportunity. As Jews we believe that Hashem requires us to carry a unique message to the world – the message of Torah. Since we have such an important message, we *must* carry ourselves with confidence on our path to serve Hashem.

If God believes in us, shouldn't we also believe in ourselves? Shouldn't we avoid the trap of loneliness and low self-esteem? Shouldn't we allow ourselves to be drawn in by the sound of the shofar?

Chapter 5
Basic Nourishment

An unusual case once came before a judge in a New Hampshire court. A man named Albert had committed a crime as a teenager which had landed him in prison. In prison, Albert reconnected to his Jewish faith and began to keep kosher. The prison allowed him to get kosher meals. But then the prison accused him of taking nonkosher chicken from the cafeteria and wanted to suspend his kosher privileges for six months.

Albert protested their decision and so the case came before a federal judge in New Hampshire. The judge admitted that he was unsure of what to do. Then he spotted in the courtroom a Chabad rabbi named Levi Krinsky. The judge ordered the rabbi to come forward and testify.

When the rabbi was in the witness stand, the judge asked him, "What do you say about such a situation?" The rabbi immediately turned to the judge and offered a *mashal* (a parable, often used in Talmudic arguments). "If a diabetic was caught eating sweets, would it be appropriate to punish him by forcing him to eat a high-sugar diet for six months?" the rabbi asked the court.

The judge quoted Rabbi Krinsky in his ruling and ordered the food to be reinstated (http://www.firstamendmentcenter.org/n-h-prison-ordered-to-restore-inmates-kosher-diet).

Just like for a regular prisoner having food is not a luxury but a necessity, so too, for a Jew having kosher food is not a luxury but a necessity. On Rosh Hashanah we read the story of another person who desperately sought food and nourishment. We read of the banishment of Yishmael, the son that Avraham had with Hagar. After Sarah gives birth to Yitzchak she tells Avraham to expel Yishmael from the house.

Avraham doesn't want to do it at first. Only after God tells him to listen to Sarah does he send away Yishmael. He gives Yishmael some bread and water and sends him on his way. But Yishmael immediately runs out of water and nearly dies in the desert. How is this possible? Why didn't Avraham just give him more water? Did Avraham drop Yishmael in the desert without enough water?

The great commentator known as Rashbam (twelfth century, northern France) defends Avraham. He notes that prior to Hagar running out of water the verse tells us that "Hagar left and wandered in the desert." Rashbam explains: "If Hagar had gone directly on the right path both she and Yishmael would have had enough water." The message is straightforward: if we wander we will lose our path and run out of water.

What is our path? Our path is the path of Hashem, and our nourishment – our water – is Torah. Water is a symbol of life *and* of Torah. If we wander from Torah, we will lose our focus in life.

How do we stay on the path of Hashem? Our responsibility is simple. We stay on the path by studying Torah, obeying the negative mitzvot, performing the positive mitzvot, and fostering a deeply intimate relationship with Hashem through, for example, prayer and acts of kindness.

If our job is so simple, why do we have such a hard time keeping the commandments? The reason is because knowing our responsibility and executing our responsibility effectively are two different things. On Rosh Hashanah we remind ourselves of what our responsibility is. It is simply to follow the Torah and the will of Hashem. The next step is to execute that responsibility. How do we follow the Torah? How do we make sure not to sin? This can be much more complicated and it requires in-depth study and ongoing commitment.

Whenever I begin a project the most important thing is to first decide my goal. Once I have a clear understanding of my goal then I can go about executing it. Rosh Hashanah is a reinforcement of our first step; it reminds us of our goal. The message of Rosh Hashanah is that we cannot wander from our path and still expect spiritual nourishment. On Rosh Hashanah we remind ourselves that just like a human being needs food, so too do we need the Torah to keep us on our path of spiritual nourishment.

In this context, the shofar is like a traffic cop's whistle. It shows us the way to go and reminds us to follow his direction. Follow the whistle and we'll be ok. The shofar of Rosh Hashanah reminds that if we follow the path of Torah, we will dwell with Hashem.

One of my favorite books is *Mesillat Yesharim*. It was written by Rabbi Moshe Chayyim Luzzatto (Ramchal), who lived in the early eighteenth century. It is a book of psychological genius, which I highly recommend everyone read during these Days of Awe. In *Mesillat Yesharim*, Ramchal tells us that life is really very simple. He begins his book with the following unusual statement:

> I have written this work not to teach people what they do not know, but rather to remind them of what they already know and clearly understand. For within most of my words you will find general words that most people know with certainty. However, to the degree that these

rules are well-known and their truth self-evident, they are routinely overlooked, or people forget about them altogether.

Ramchal then goes on to remind us of this simple message: the path to Hashem is to follow the Torah with humility and to constantly remind ourselves that this is our goal. The essence of our responsibility and duty in life is not hard to understand.

Thus, one message of the Rosh Hashanah Torah reading is that we need to stay on our path of Torah. Don't lose focus. We should be reminding ourselves of this every day, but at the very least we remind ourselves of this every year on Rosh Hashanah as we refocus and return to the basics.

But if that is all Rosh Hashanah is for us then we are missing the point. The Torah reading also teaches us another lesson about nourishment. After Avraham expels Yishmael from his home, the Torah relates that Avraham settles down and plants an *eshel* and calls out in the name of God. An *eshel* is literally an orchard. Why is Avraham planting an orchard and what does that have to do with calling out in the name of Hashem?

Rashi explains that the *eshel* was a *pundak* – an inn for travelers. It is as though Avraham realized his error of letting Yishmael wander on the path and run out of water and so what he does now is a type of *teshuvah*. Avraham builds an orchard or an inn to make sure that no traveler will run out of water. If someone has wandered off the path then Avraham will help them and resuscitate them.

Avraham sets up an *eshel* – a guesthouse to help the wanderers. He recognizes that it is his responsibility to make sure that people do not wander. But he also recognizes that the best way for him not to lose the path and for his family members not to lose the path is to set up a guesthouse. His own family members will better understand their mission if they are teaching it to others.

The model of the *eshel* is a second lesson of Rosh Hashanah and it is an important lesson for every synagogue. A synagogue needs to be an *eshel*, a place where spiritual wanderers can find a home, where anyone can stop in and receive nourishment. If we make our synagogues into *eshelim* then others who wander will be nourished by us. If we create *eshelim*, we will be helping others on their spiritual journeys. And if we help others we will be strengthening ourselves.

A young family once moved to my community after studying in Pardes, an institute in Israel that trains Jewish educators. Sometimes when people move into a community they ask, "What can I get out of this community?" That is an important question but it is not enough. Within a week of moving in this family approached me and said, "How can we help? How can we volunteer and teach on behalf of the community?" And so, they began leading two Hebrew classes a week, offering their services as tutors to people in need, helping out with the youth on Shabbat, teaching at a women's *beit midrash*, organizing a communal night of Torah study, and starting a beginners service for people who needed help getting adjusted to synagogue.

They obviously have more skills then many others, but their model should be an inspirational model for all of us. We all have something to teach and to offer. We all have unique experiences. For example, only one who has entered the synagogue not knowing how to read Hebrew can really relate to someone else who walks in not knowing how to read Hebrew. Our unique experience just might be the *eshel* that others need to find their path.

It may sound funny, but this is the reason why every year I go with two people from my congregation who are dressed up like a bee and an apple and give out honey on the streets of downtown D.C. It all comes from the same approach. A community needs to let people know about its *eshel*.

We can only grow stronger if we all assume the responsibility of building an *eshel*. By turning our homes and our synagogues and our skills into guest homes for wandering Jews, we stay on the path. For when we welcome wanderers in, and teach them, they in turn remind us of our need to stay on the path.

Personally, my spirituality is enhanced when I teach Torah. When I teach I get energized and excited. When I watch someone else do a mitzvah for the first time, I get a spiritual high that I can't always reach as I perform the mitzvah for the umpteenth time. When I build an *eshel* I am the one who is most nourished.

Rosh Hashanah should be a call to challenge ourselves: We must also try to build a personal *eshel*. If we build an *eshel* for others to find their path then our own paths will be that much brighter.

Chapter 6
Can You Hear Me Now?

For a couple of years I had the opportunity of accompanying one of my children on frequent visits to the ENT. We had always thought our son simply wasn't listening to us when we were talking to him. He kept saying, "What'd you say?" But in the end I was really the one not listening properly, or I would have noticed earlier that he needed tubes in his ears to help him hear better.

My *oma* also had trouble hearing. I remember one time, just a couple of years before she passed away, when she went to her ENT for a visit. The doctor said in a very loud voice, "Mrs. Herzfeld, can you hear me?" Without missing a beat, she said, "Doctor, if I could hear you, would I be here?"

One of the frustrating things about modern technology is trying to use a cell phone. The call comes in and you get excited to talk with the person, but then invariably you spend the next few minutes of the call struggling to hear the other person. You end up walking around saying, "Can you hear me now?" That line – "Can you hear me now" – should be the motto of Rosh Hashanah. It should be placed on the front page of every siddur and on the entrance of every synagogue.

On Rosh Hashanah we are commanded to hear, *"lishmoa kol shofar"* (to hear the sound of the shofar). The sound of the shofar is majestic and awe inspiring. According to the Talmud (*Rosh Hashanah* 30a), it seems that the original custom was that every person in the synagogue would blow the shofar on Rosh Hashanah. Says the Talmud, "When the leader finished his blasts in the city of Yavneh, a person could not hear any sound in his ear, because of the noise of the shofar blasts of all the private individuals." Eventually this custom gave way to our current custom of having one person blow the shofar for everyone. Presumably the custom was changed because when everyone blasted the shofar together it sounded like the Jewish people were going out to fight a war. It is certainly a very different mood today. Instead of everyone blowing the shofar together, we have one person representing all of us in the middle of the room.

As the shofar blower stands up to blow we all lean forward; everyone is tense and excited. Why the tension?

Musically, it is just a simple note which can easily be reproduced. But we recognize that when we sound the shofar we are not just making music. We are bringing God's voice into the world. The shofar is the sound of Hashem calling us.

The question to ponder on Rosh Hashanah thus becomes: If God is calling us with the sound of the shofar, what is He asking us to do? What is He saying to us?

To answer this question let's turn to the Torah reading for the first day of Rosh Hashanah. Hashem remembers the elderly Sarah, after decades of barrenness, and blesses her with a child. Overflowing with joy, Sarah exclaims, *"Kol hashomea yitzachak li"* (Whoever will hear will be happy for me; Bereishit 21:6).

This is the traditional way to read the verse. But perhaps we can read it another way as well. The word *hashomeah* is spelled *hey – shin – mem – ayin* (ה-ש-מ-ע). So it can also be vocalized as *haShema*, or "the Shema!" In other words, whoever heeds the words of the Shema will be happy with me.

The Shema is the clarion call to have faith in *Hakadosh barukh Hu*. Throughout the centuries, as Jews were being martyred, they shouted out the words of Shema and declared their inextinguishable faith in God.

This verse is designated by the rabbis as a central part of our liturgy. It is selected by the rabbis to conclude the section of Musaf known as Malchiyot (Kingship).

During her barren years, Sarah's faith had been tested. Sarah had originally doubted God's plan. She thought she and her husband were too old for children. She thought it would never happen. But now that God had remembered her, Sarah declares her gratitude to Hashem for making others happy as well. God had remembered not only Sarah, but also all those who had faith in Him.

Indeed, Rashi explains that everyone was happy for Sarah because on that day not only were Sarah's prayers answered, but also many others who were in distress were delivered on that day: "Many barren women were remembered, many sick were healed, and many prayers were answered."

On Rosh Hashanah, Sarah's experience reminds us that we too should use our faith to help us seek out Hashem. We believe that He will be with us in our moments of need and that He will hold our hand when we need Him most. God remembered Sarah, and others of her generation. And no matter how distant salvation seems for us, we pray that He will also remember us. We will not give up hope in the possibility of salvation.

With this understanding we can learn a deep lesson of the shofar. The blessing recited on the shofar is "to hear [*lishmoa*] the sound of the shofar." What are we hearing? We are hearing the commandment of the Shema to have faith in Hashem. Every time we hear the shofar blast on Rosh Hashanah we are reminding ourselves to follow the message of the Shema to come closer to God, to believe in Hashem with all our heart and soul.

But how can we be commanded to have faith in Hashem? For many people it seems so distant and so difficult.

Some people have a mistaken impression of me. Some people have said to me, "Faith comes so easy for you, while for me it is difficult." Some people assume that it is easy for me to have faith in God because I am a rabbi or that I became a rabbi because my faith in God was so strong. They then say, "But for me it is so difficult to have faith in God. What can I do?"

Let me clarify this point with a story about myself when I was in my last year of college. A bunch of my fellow students had gathered for a meeting with one of the great rabbis of our generation, Rabbi Shlomo Riskin. All of us in that room were seriously thinking of becoming rabbis and Rabbi Riskin went around the room asking us why we were interested in the rabbinate.

Friend after friend listed inspiring moments in their lives that had turned them on to the rabbinate. When it came to be my turn, I was nervous. How was I going to explain that my faith was not as rock solid as those of my friends? I told Rabbi Riskin that I was interested in pursuing the rabbinate not because I was interested in becoming a congregational rabbi, but because I was struggling with my faith. Since I was struggling I wanted to learn more about my faith and so I planned on studying Torah day and night in a rigorous curriculum.

Rabbi Riskin said to me, "Becoming a rabbi is a great way to overcome struggles with your faith. The more you study and you teach, the more you give over, the stronger your faith will become."

Looking back now, more than two decades later, I realize how true his words were. I feel that today I am so much stronger in my faith in Hashem. I attribute my increased strength to my life as a rabbi. The more I teach Torah, the stronger my faith becomes. The more I teach, the more connected I feel to Hashem and to His protection.

Benjamin Franklin once said, "If you want someone to like you, don't do a favor for them – ask them to do a favor for you." The more we give, the more we love the one we give to. The same is true about acquiring more faith in God. The more we teach Torah, the more faith we acquire and the closer we become to God.

We have spoken about one meaning of the shofar: the call from Hashem to have greater faith in God and to believe in His ways. But the Torah in parashat Behaalotekha tells us about another idea: "When a battle comes into your midst, you should blast the trumpets" (Bamidbar 10:9). In this understanding, the shofar is a call to battle, a call to arms. We should adopt that meaning as well – not as a call to a physical battle, but to a spiritual battle. The sound of the shofar should inspire us to enroll in the army of God as His servants, to serve by being His teachers and His emissaries.

And if we can't all be teachers of Torah (although I believe we all *can* be), we can each commit to doing something tangible. Find something you can invest yourself in – a way of giving to the world.

One time I met a lawyer who was involved in a landmark disability court case. As a result of his lawsuit a judge literally changed the world for the better. The lawyer who sued the government and won was a solo practitioner who did the entire case pro bono. I asked him why he had done it. He told me that he had once had a friend with this disability; he took on this case as a way of giving honor to his friend and giving even more meaning to his life. We should all look to adopt that model. Find a way in which we can work to transform the world.

The ancient custom of having everyone in the congregation blast the shofar sends a powerful message. The more we each blast our shofar the closer we each come to God. But we do not have to physically blast the actual shofar; we can do so in a metaphoric manner as well. Whether to our children, our relatives, our friends, or our coworkers, we should all seek out opportunities to enroll in this army and spread the message of Hashem. If we do so, our faith will grow infinitely stronger.

The blast of the shofar asks us to hear God and to hear His call, to have faith in His promises. It also asks us to blast our own shofar right back at Hashem. Only by blasting our own shofar can we really, truly hear Hashem's call.

Chapter 7
The Story of Chanah: From Loneliness to Community

Who do you think is the loneliest person in Jewish history?

In my opinion the answer is Elisha ben Avuyah, also known as Acher (Other). The Talmud (*Chagigah* 15a) tells us the following story. Elisha ben Avuyah was at one point in his life one of the greatest rabbis of his generation. But then he had a dangerous mystical vision of God that led him astray. He envisioned heaven as having a duality – a theological no-no – and this affected his belief in Hashem's oneness. And so he became a heretic.

The Talmud says that Elisha heard a heavenly voice declare, "*Shuvu, banim shovavim – chutz me'Acher*" (Repent, My wayward children – except for Acher). Everyone except for Acher has a chance to repent. When Elisha heard that the whole world could repent except for him he said, "I might as well live it up in this world." And so, figuring that he has already lost his share in the World to Come, he goes and visits a harlot. When the harlot sees him, she declares, "I cannot accept your business for you are the great rabbi, Elisha ben Avuyah." But Elisha ben Avuyah wants to prove to the harlot that he is no longer a pious Jew, so he purposely violates the Shabbat in front of her. When she sees this she says, "You are no longer Elisha ben Avuyah. From now on you are Acher [Other]."

A basic principle of Rosh Hashanah and Yom Kippur is that everyone has the ability to repent. So why is Elisha being denied the opportunity? And why does the harlot call him Acher?

Even though Elisha had renounced his faith and had become a heretic, he still could not leave his past life of piety behind. The Talmud tells us that he would still engage in discussions with his former student, Rabbi Meir. At the same time Elisha clearly felt estranged from God.

He became a heretic, but he still remained with one foot in the world of believers. He couldn't fit in with anyone. Even the harlot – a person without an identity, estranged from society – even she did not accept him. This is why the harlot calls him Acher. He did not fit in anywhere in this world. He was an Other.

But ultimately his loneliness came from the fact that he was distant from God. At one point Elisha had been so close to Hashem. He had entered into supremely advanced mystical visions. But then he grew distant from God. He grew apart. Distance from God is the ultimate loneliness in this world. There can be no greater loneliness than distance from Hashem.

There comes a time in the lives of many people when they wake up and suddenly realize that they are lonely. They might be surrounded by many family members and great friends, but their lives are without direction. They awaken to the fact that they are not alone, but they are incredibly lonely.

It is true that many people have friends and family to turn to. But at the end of the day there is a pervasive loneliness that casts its shadow over human existence. Rabbi Soloveitchik describes this experience in *Worship of the Heart*, as the realization that we stand in total isolation in the world (Rabbi Joseph B. Soloveitchik, *Worship of the Heart: Essays on Jewish Prayer*, ed. Shalom Carmy [NY: Ktav, 2003], 78–83).

In his formulation, on the one hand we exist in a natural world – the world of science – which is overwhelming in its greatness. But for many people the greatness of the natural world does not necessarily draw us closer to God as much as it intimidates us. We feel like a paean, a speck in the world, all alone in a world that appears to run almost mechanically.

History, too, serves to further our isolation. The historical world, Rabbi Soloveitchik argues, does not seem to be bringing us closer to a utopian future. Instead we are just moving farther and farther away from our dreams. We are left to flail helplessly and question the nature of human existence.

This reality is perhaps the main problem that I see in the lives of people who are floundering spiritually. In conversation after conversation with people in my rabbinate, I sense a pervasive sadness stemming from the recognition that there is something missing in their lives. Aristotle taught us that man is a social animal; we need to move beyond our loneliness in order to exist. A core question in our lives is: How do we move beyond our isolation and loneliness?

The haftarah for the first day of Rosh Hashanah provides two answers to this question. The haftarah tells us of a man named Elkanah who has two wives: Chanah and Peninah. Peninah has many children, but Chanah is childless. When we first meet Chanah she is the definition of a lonely person. We are told, "*l'Chanah ein yeladim*" (Chanah has no children). It is as though her last name is "no children." She is defined by the absence of a relationship.

Chanah is depressed and bitter and, despite the fact that she has a loving husband, she is lonely. She wants no part in the world. Her husband says to her, "Why are you crying? Why are you not eating? Why is your heart bitter?" (1 Shmuel 1:8).

But Chanah ultimately transcends her loneliness, and she manages to do so through prayer. The Talmud tells us that Chanah's prayer to Hashem is the source of how we should all pray. The reason is that Chanah revolutionizes prayer. She prays to Hashem like we speak to a friend. She speaks to Him directly. She calls Him by the name Hashem Tzevakot, and no one had ever been able to do that before her. Chanah pours out her heart before Hashem like we would speak only to the closest of our friends – she says *"me'rov sichi v'khaasi dibarti ad henah"* (I have spoken from a place of great pain).

Before Chanah spoke to Hashem in this manner, no one would have dared to talk to God so familiarly. But Chanah not only revolutionizes *how* to pray, she also revolutionizes the concept of prayer. Through the words of her prayer Chanah is able to form a connection, a friendship with Hashem. She pierces through the loneliness and creates an eternal relationship. She didn't just pray once – she prayed incessantly. As the verse says, "Chanah prayed heavily before Hashem."

When you pray to Hashem you are recognizing that you are not alone in this world. This is the power of prayer. It offers you companionship with your Maker; it offers a path toward ending the loneliness. It creates a community of two – you and God.

This yearning for a real friendship with God is found in the words of psalm 27, which we say morning and evening in the High Holiday season. We cry, "I request only one thing from Hashem: to dwell in His house forever!" and, "Though my father and mother will forsake me, You, Hashem, will gather me in." When we take prayer seriously we have the potential to form a lasting friendship with Hashem. It is a relationship that will end the loneliness and guide us at all times.

The second way to break through our existential loneliness can also be learned from the actions of Chanah. When Chanah prays to Hashem for a child, she promises that if a child would be born to her she would dedicate him for service to Hashem. She doesn't confine her life to prayer only. When her son is born, she says, "I will now lend my son to Hashem for his whole life" (1 Shmuel 1:28).

The path to ending loneliness is to involve oneself in the service of Hashem. In some ways service is different than prayer, but in other ways it is a type of prayer. If prayer is worship of the heart, then service is the worship of the hands and legs. Service to Hashem can mean filling a task on behalf of a spiritual community, or it can mean performing acts of kindness and good deeds on behalf of others. This second path to ending loneliness begins by helping others. When we help others we will feel a closer friendship with Hashem and will no longer be lonely in this world.

The Hebrew word for repent is *teshuvah*, which literally means "return." The reason that Elisha ben Avuya could not repent is because he was Other, Acher. He could not figure out how to transcend his loneliness. Rather than pray, he went to visit a harlot; rather than serve others he sought to serve himself – to live it up before he died. And so he died a lonely man.

I once had an experience that taught me both of these lessons. On June 10, 2009, an anti-Semite seeking to commit an evil act and inflict great pain on people attacked the United States Holocaust Memorial Museum in Washington, D.C. The security guard at the museum, a brave man named Stephen Johns, acted heroically and prevented the attacker from doing more damage. Tragically, Officer Stephen Johns was murdered in the attack. Soon after the attack I went with Rabbi Avi Weiss and Rabbi Tamara Miller to visit with Kiah Johns, the wife of Officer Johns. We were joined that morning by Kiah's grandfather and her minister.

We sat in the presence of a grieving widow. Just by looking at her face I could tell how lonely she was. Since the death of Stephen, she had been surrounded by cameras and friends and family. But she was lonely, a young wife without her husband.

I said that we were there to offer words of support. Her pastor asked me to recite a prayer, so we all held hands and I did recite a prayer. And we all cried together.

And then she said, "I do not want Stephen to be remembered as only a security guard. That was just a part of him. He was so much more. He was fun and loving. He was joyful and loving. He brought light to so many people." And so we resolved that we would do an act of service together as a community – bringing my congregation together with his church – in service of Hashem. And, of course, I invited her to come and pray with my congregation sometime as well.

By the end of the meeting, I do not think we took away her pain, but I am hopeful that her loneliness was diminished.

That is what we should all resolve to accomplish. We will not share the fate of Elisha ben Avuyah. We will not die from loneliness. We will pray to Hashem with more fervor and develop a real friendship with Him. And we will dedicate ourselves to the service of Hashem by helping others. And if we do that we will experience a real renewal on Rosh Hashanah.

Chapter 8
Mirror Image

It is easier to see something incorrectly than to change the way we see.

My vision used to be -9. So I had surgery and my vision changed to 20/15. The whole surgery took less than five minutes. So I now have 20/15 vision, but as some people close to me keep reminding me: I might have perfect vision, but I still often miss what I am supposed to be looking at.

"*Ki hamitzvah hazot asher anokhi metzavekha hayom lo nifleit hi mimkha v'lo rechokah hi*" (For this mitzvah that I command you today is not too difficult for you and it is not distant from you; Devarim 30:11). Nachmanides teaches us that this verse is a reference to the mitzvah of *teshuvah* (repentance). It is not distant from us; it is right under our eyes at all times. We just have to be willing to open our eyes and look.

One summer I had a lesson in opening my eyes. Our shul runs a summer camp called Camp Kibbutz. It is great fun and as part of the fun we manage to sneak in some education as well. This particular summer the theme of the camp was about the importance of and the need to recite blessings (*berakhot*). So every time we did something fun and special we managed to find the appropriate blessing to recite.

As part of the camp we went to see the Luray Caverns in the Shenandoah Valley. It was an unbelievable subterranean display of natural beauty. It is a natural wonder and so, of course, I can't describe it adequately. But visiting these caverns is an incredible experience.

The story of how these beautiful caverns were discovered is amazing. The caverns are said to be 450 million years old, but they were only discovered on August 13, 1878. That's when a local tinsmith named Andrew Campbell felt some cool air coming from the ground, so he dug away some rocks and found a cavern. In fact he had discovered one of the largest series of caverns in the United States.

Our camp gathered together in the dark caverns and we recited the blessing one makes over a natural wonder, "*Oseh maaseh bereishit*." I said to the campers that the amazing thing was that these caverns had been there for 450 million years and no one had noticed them. For 450 million years there was a beautiful site that today is visited by more than five hundred thousand people a year, and no one noticed it! 450 million years! How is that possible?!

It is possible because it is often the case that we can't see what is right in front of our own eyes.

On the first day of Rosh Hashanah, we read that after Avraham had banished Hagar from his household she went into the desert. After all of her water was used up, she moved away from her child so that she wouldn't see him die. Abandoning all hope of being saved, she lifted up her voice and began to cry. God heard the cries of her son, Yishmael, and He had pity. Says the Torah, "Hashem opened her eyes, and she saw a well of water" (Bereishit 21:19).

The commentators explain that God did not miraculously create the well of water at that moment for Hagar. All He did was open up her eyes so that she could see it. The water had been there the whole time – she just couldn't see it.

We too are often like Hagar, unable to see what is right in front of our eyes. Why couldn't Hagar see that day in the desert? The reason is because she was depressed and pessimistic. What we see in this world is a reflection of who we are. We see a mirror image of what we are. Psychologists might call this projection, but it is really a Torah-true idea that is central to the concept of *teshuvah*.

Hagar couldn't see her salvation because she was convinced that she was about to die. She needed God's help to allow her to see. This is one of the most powerful reasons to have a relationship with God. God allows us to open our eyes and to see that the answer is already in front of us; we just need to change our perspective. This is a potent message for Rosh Hashanah. On the birthday of the world, we need to remember that God has already given us all our answers; we just need to open our eyes and look.

But there is another lesson that we can take from the Hagar story. And this is a lesson that directly impacts on how we can change for the better. What we see is a reflection of who we are; that is certainly true. But the converse is also true: if we want to change who we are *then we need to start seeing others the way we want to be seen*!

This is the key to *teshuvah*: in order to change we need to change the way we see the world and the way we see others. We need to see the best in people; judge them for merit (*"hevei dan et kol ha'adam l'khaf zekhut"*) and then we too will change and be judged for merit.

I once heard a similar idea from a friend of mine. There is a concept in Judaism that every generation has thirty-six hidden tzaddikim – *lamed-vavnikim* – who uphold the world with their righteousness. These hidden tzaddikim are inspirational – but people can't see them even though they are right in front of their eyes.

My friend explained: The secret of the *lamed-vavnikim* is that they are your mirror. If you look at them and think they are obnoxious or ugly, it is because you are obnoxious and ugly. If you look at them and think they are holy, then it is because you are holy. They reflect who you are.

Only if we are truly righteous will we be able to see the greatness of the *lamed vavnikim*, otherwise, we will merely see ourselves! The *lamed vavnikim* are hidden from us, because we are not able to recognize their greatness.

This same idea is reflected in the Torah and haftarah readings for the first day of Rosh Hashanah. We read the stories of two barren women who are both righteous and pure: Sarah and Chanah. The Torah tells us, "*Hashem pakad et Sarah*" (God remembered Sarah). Sarah desperately wanted a child, and God answered her prayers and gave her a child named Yitzchak.

And in the haftarah we read a similar story about Chanah. Chanah is married to Elkanah and she desperately wants a child. So she prays to God in a powerful way, unlike she or anyone else has ever prayed before, and Hashem answers her prayers. In the end, she gives birth to a child named Shmuel.

Today, the issue of infertility struggles is an extremely sensitive and painful one affecting many people. Some studies show that more than 25 percent of couples have difficulty conceiving a child. And for the couple trying to conceive it is often a lonely struggle.

This theme is a very painful one. It was then, and it is now. So we wonder, why did our rabbis select these particular passages as the scriptural readings for this very holy day?

It is because these barren women, Sarah and Chanah, can teach us how to do *teshuvah*. Not, God forbid, because a barren women is an example of someone who has sinned. Just the opposite! It is because a barren woman represents someone standing before God with a purity and nobleness that should inspire us all. When we desire to repent, we too need to come to Hashem and throw ourselves at His feet with pure prayers and noble intentions. In order to be able to return to Hashem properly – to do a *teshuvah gemurah* – we must make sure that our prayers are as pure and our intentions as noble as a person seeking a child.

So Chanah and Sarah represented people who were praying with the purest of hearts and intentions. But do you think that the world was able to see that?

Not a chance!

Says the book of Shmuel, Chanah was sitting there praying from the depths of her heart, *hi medaberet al libah*, and the high priest, the leader of the Jewish people, Eli, thought she was a drunk! Chanah was pure, but Eli couldn't see her purity; he saw only a drunkard. And it's no wonder that once Shmuel was finally born, Eli was unable to hear the voice of God, whereas Shmuel heard the voice as a young boy.

The key to coming close to Hashem is seeing what's in front of our eyes and seeing the greatness of others. Let's say you don't think that the people sitting next to you in shul are so great – then push yourself a little bit and try to find their greatest qualities. Look for their greatness and you will find it. And then it will transform you and eventually you will morph into greatness as well.

The *Kedushat Levi*, Reb Levi Yitzchak of Berditchev, teaches this same idea as it relates to Hashem. King David says in psalm 121, "*Hashem tzilkha al yad yeminekha*" (Hashem is your shadow on your right hand). Reb Levi Yitzchak explains that this means that Hashem is your reflection; whatever you are feeling is what you will see as God. If you are an ugly and bitter person, then that is what you will see in other people and in Hashem.

The challenge of Rosh Hashanah is for us to understand that a relationship with God is not distant from us at all. *Teshuvah* – the ability to repent and change our lives for the better – is what will bring us to that relationship. *Teshuvah* is right under our eyes, but we must be willing to open our eyes and look. Then we will notice the greatness in others and in ourselves as well. Once we begin to see the greatness of others, we too will become great and we will not be distant – not from our friends, not from ourselves, and not from Hashem.

Chapter 9
A Reinvigorated Evangelical Jew

Once there was a very nice article about me in an online magazine. By that I mean it said very nice things about me, but it had at least one mistake. It said I was the rabbi of Ohev Sholom, located in Dupont Circle.

This is an honest mistake since I do spend some time on the streets of downtown D.C. Before every holiday I try to spend a few hours and be a physical presence on the streets of the city. I have been doing this for a few years now so I have a relationship with the people there. I know the homeless man who asks for extra honey on Rosh Hashanah, and extra chocolate on Chanukah, but doesn't like the taste of matzah on Pesach.

But I don't go to Dupont Circle. Instead I go to the corner of Connecticut and K since advertisers know that that is the busiest intersection of the city. And what I am doing is advertising our religion.

The article also called me an evangelist. This, I'll admit, is true. I am an evangelical rabbi. There are two main reasons why I evangelize and try to bring Jews closer to Judaism. First, I love Hashem so much that I want to share the love I feel with others. And second, I learn so much from the people I encounter when I evangelize. The more I evangelize, the more inspired I become.

It is often the person who appears to be the farthest away from Judaism who can turn around in an instant and teach me a great deal about Torah. They will have an insight or a thought that inspires me and illuminates my own spirituality. So I engage Jews who are far away from traditional Orthodoxy in order to share my love of Torah, but also in order to learn at their feet. Just because these Jews don't observe the Torah the way I do, doesn't mean that they can't illuminate my relationship with the Torah.

Elisha ben Avuyah was a great rabbi from the Talmud, who became a heretic. He was a very lonely and isolated man who had sinned so greatly that he was no longer called by his name, but instead was called Acher, or "the other." But there is a beautiful story about him in the Talmud (*Chagigah* 15a). The Talmud tells us: "Once Acher was riding on his horse on Shabbat and Rabbi Meir was following behind him on foot to learn Torah from his mouth."

This is a shocking story! Rabbi Meir was a great rabbi and he was following behind Acher on Shabbat – while Acher was literally violating Shabbat – in order to learn Torah from Acher. Acher wasn't just "distant" from Hashem; he was perceived as the supreme heretic of his time. The Talmud goes so far as to say that Hashem says everyone's name except for Acher's, And yet here is Rabbi Meir following behind him, studying the Torah while Acher is publicly violating the Sabbath.

The message for me is simple. We must be ready and willing to study Torah from everyone, even from people who are heretics, and even from people who we perceive to be "off the path." Just because Acher was a heretic does not mean that we cannot learn at his feet.

The Talmud further tells us that when Acher died, there was a debate in heaven about whether or not he could enter into the next world. And so a great rabbi on this earth, Rabbi Yochanan, said, "When I die, I will lead him by my hand." Rabbi Yochanan is teaching us that ultimately we are intertwined with Acher. We must learn from him and when we have nothing to learn from him, then we must lead him by the hand. One day when we get to the next world we will bear responsibility for him.

We have a communal responsibility as it relates to the *acherim* – the others – of the world. This can mean reaching out to the unengaged Jews of the world: bringing in those distant Jews who claim to be atheists, or who are still scarred by a bad Hebrew school experience that they once had. As Rabbi Yochanan and Rabbi Meir teach us, they are all our responsibility.

But engaging Acher does not only mean reaching out. Sometimes there are *acherim* who live right next to us, daven right next to us, and are somehow disengaged from the faith. They are often great Jews who are just in a spiritual slump. This too is part of our responsibility. It is to reach in – inside our community – and make sure that those who we pray and study with are spiritually engaged in a meaningful manner.

This concept of reaching out to Acher is so fundamental to our faith that it dominates our liturgy on Rosh Hashanah. The Musaf of Rosh Hashanah has three special additional sections to the Amidah, and the first one is called Malkhiyot, or Kingship. In the section of Malkhiyot, we praise God as King of the universe. But what we are really doing is not just declaring that God is the King, but rather praying for the entire world to *recognize* that God is King of the universe. As we declare in one of the most famous *piyyutim* of Rosh Hashanah: "*V'yishmeu rechokim va'yavo'u v'yitnu lekha keter melukhah!*" (And all the distant people will hear and come close and place upon your head the crown of Kingship!). On Rosh Hashanah we pray for the distant people to recognize God as King.

Thus, reaching out to the *acherim* of the world is axiomatic to our faith and fundamental to our prayers. But truth be told, sometimes I just don't want to be an evangelist. Sometimes I don't want to share the love of Hashem with others. Sometimes I just want to focus on my own spirituality.

But once you are an evangelist it is more difficult to do that. One time I was telling one of my younger children that I needed to go to shul. This child wanted me to stay home a little bit longer. But I insisted that I needed to go to shul. So the child asked me, "Why do you have to go?" I was about to say "Because I need to daven to Hashem," when he blurted out, "I know why you need to go. You need to call out the pages!"

I don't mind calling out the pages, but sometimes I really want to daven and the evangelism gets in the way.

I remember one morning when I was intent on really working on my davening. I had read an inspirational passage about prayer and I wanted to just immerse myself in the words of the liturgy. That morning, I washed my hands before prayers with special intensity. I put my *tallit* and *tefillin* on with great *kavvanah*. And I began to recite the words of the davening. I was having a great spiritual moment. I felt really connected to the words and I was flying high.

But just then someone came and asked me if I had an extra pair of *tefillin*. "Of course," I said, "let me get it for you. Let me show you how to put it on." And then after I was able to help this person, another person arrived and they too sought help, and then I was distracted again.

Now on the one hand, I just love helping people put *tefillin* on. I love watching the intensity and excitement that people have for the mitzvah. On the other hand, that morning I just wanted to pray in my own space before Hashem.

There were some rabbis in the Talmud who were very upset with Rabbi Meir for following after Elisha ben Avuyah. They felt that he had made a big mistake. And I understand that criticism. If we are always focusing on Acher and his ilk, then we are unable to absorb the Torah ourselves. Believe me, I know this to be true as well. One of the great challenges of the rabbinate is finding time to remember who you are: to absorb your own Torah while you are in the middle of teaching others.

This idea of remembering who we once were is contained in the second additional section of the Rosh Hashanah Musaf: Zikhronot, or Remembrances. In this section we call upon Hashem to remember us not as we are now, but as we once were. *"Zakharti lakh chesed ne'urayikh"* (I remember the kindness of your youth).

If Malkhiyot is a challenge for us to engage the world, Zikhronot is a challenge to reengage ourselves, to return to the relationship we once had with Hashem. If Malkhiyot is a challenge for our community to engage the "other," Zikhronot is a reminder that we as individuals and as a community need to reengage ourselves. It is a reminder not to focus so much on the *"acherim"* that we forget who we are as well.

That is what this section of the service is telling us: *"Zakharti Ani et briti otakh bi'yemei ne'urayikh"* (I remember My covenant with you in the days of your youth). Hashem is telling us and we are declaring back to Him that while we are busy getting the whole world to remember that He is king, we must not forget that He has a special covenant with each of us.

Malkhiyot and Zikhronot are teaching us two different but important ideas about where to focus our energy. We might wonder which we should do first: Should we focus on engaging others or should we focus on reengaging ourselves?

The answer lies in the third additional section to the Musaf: Shofarot. In Shofarot we pray for the utopian world to come into existence; we pray for the messianic era.

The shofar is a prayer that speaks to all Jews. It is a simple musical instrument; it is a prayer without words that is accessible to all. But it is a powerful prayer, perhaps the most powerful prayer of all. When we are able to live and embrace the teachings of Malkhiyot and Zikhronot then we will be able to fully sound the shofar. We declare in Shofarot, *"V'hayah bayom hahu yitaka b'shofar gadol u'va'u ha'ovdim..."* – On that day a great shofar will be blown and the distant ones will come close and bow down to Hashem on the Temple Mount.

What a scene that will be on the Temple Mount. All the distant Jews from around the world will join the Jews already praying every day at the Temple Mount and they will hear the shofar together. The sound of that shofar blast is the messianic shofar; the powerful energy of trying to get the whole world to crown the king and at the same time remember who we are is what creates the messianic era.

This is a challenge for each of us as individuals and as members of a community. It is a difficult challenge, but it is one we must embrace.

For the Jews of the desert the sound of the shofar was a unifying sound. It was a call to pick up their tents and start out on their journey. For us, too, it must be a call to march, to invigorate ourselves and to bring about the conflicting visions of *both engaging ourselves and engaging the world.*

And so I want to share with you a vision of what that fulfillment might look like. The following is a letter I got a decade ago from someone from my shul in response to his attendance at one of the shul's programs:

> Without having attended a few of the "Developmentally Different" events such as the pizza dinner and such, I would still be scared of those with Down's syndrome.... By being around, I have become a participant instead of an onlooker. I volunteered to sing songs during Chanukah, and then I took a resident of another home to a puppet show.... Perhaps I have now found my niche.

This person then went on to dedicate his life professionally to helping people with special needs. At the time he wrote the letter he was looking for his niche. But by giving to others he discovered who he was meant to be.

We can all find our niche. But to do so we must crown Hashem as King and reinvigorate ourselves, and then we can all march together on our journey!

Chapter 10
The Obligations of Man and the Mercy of God

The great early-medieval philosopher and rabbi, Rav Saadyah Gaon (Baghdad, d. 942), tackles the question that should occupy all of us every year on the *Yamim Noraim*. Rosh Hashanah is the day we commemorate the birth of the world and the day of judgment for all of the world's creatures. Why is it that the central prayer chosen to symbolize our day is the simple blast of the shofar?

Rav Saadyah offers ten separate explanations for why we blow a shofar on Rosh Hashanah (cited in the fourteenth-century Spanish work *Abudraham*, 269–270). I find three of his suggestions especially compelling. One reason offered is that since Rosh Hashanah is really the birthday of the creation of the world, we blow the shofar in order to commemorate the start of God's sovereignty over this universe. Just like when a king used to begin his rule, the coronation ceremony would begin with trumpet blasts, so too, we recall the coronation of God in the universe by blasting our shofarot, our horns. In doing so we are signaling that we accept God's rule over our lives.

A second reason suggested is that the shofar blasts should cause us to recall that moment in time when we accepted the Torah. When the Jewish people were gathered at the foot of Mount Sinai, they were accompanied by the sounds of strong shofar blasts. And so we blow the shofar on Rosh Hashanah to remind us of how we accepted the Torah at Sinai and how we should always affirm our commitment to the Sinaitic revelation.

A third reason for blowing the shofar on Rosh Hashanah relates to us on a personal level. The shofar is a siren intended to awaken us from our slumber and inspire us to repent – to do *teshuvah* before God. And so we blast the shofar to signal us: Tremble before God! Repent properly!

Rav Saadyah continues and offers another seven explanations. Yet in truth, all ten explanations revolve around a single theme. And that theme is not just the theme of the shofar but is really the theme of all of Rosh Hashanah. The theme of all of these explanations is that *the shofar should remind us of our obligations to God.*

The shofar blast is a siren, to which we react in fear and trembling. Yet we remind ourselves on Rosh Hashanah that we cannot be paralyzed. We are *obligated* to repent and to entirely accept the dominion of God over us. The shofar bids us tremble before the King Who created us, the King Who commands us to follow His laws, the King Who commands us to repent for our sins.

The shofar symbolizes our obligations before the Almighty, the Master of the universe: Commit everything that we have at all times to our God. Return fully to God. And that is what Rosh Hashanah is about. It's about us doing *teshuvah* and accepting our responsibilities before our Master. It is about us declaring that we will not shirk our religious and social obligations. If we do fail in these areas, we will have to stand before the King of the universe.

There is, however, one difficulty with Rav Saadyah's approach. Rav Saadyah's explanations work to explain the piercing siren-like blast of the *tekiah*, but they don't account for the softer, more staccato sound of the *teruah*.

In order to understand the sound of the *teruah*, let us compare the symbol of Rosh Hashanah – the shofar – with what is in many ways the symbol of Yom Kippur – the book of Yonah. Why do we read and study the book of Yonah on Yom Kippur? Many scholars argue that we read this text on the afternoon of Yom Kippur precisely because this work demonstrates the concept of *teshuvah* – that God will forgive us if we repent for our sins, just like God rescinded His harsh decree and forgave the Ninevites who repented for their sins. And according to this explanation, the book of Yonah reflects the same theme as the blast on Rosh Hashanah. It is our obligation to repent before God and we are reminded to do so before it is too late.

However, there is a major obstacle with the approach that sees the central message of Yonah as a call to repentance. The problem is a textual one. If we read the text of Yonah carefully, only chapter 3 (the chapter in which the Ninevites actually repent) focuses on the concept of *teshuvah*. And if the book really were about *teshuvah* then there would be no need for a fourth chapter. The fact that the book doesn't end with chapter 3 shows us that *teshuvah* is not the central message.

In fact, a careful reading of the text shows that the Ninevites don't even perform a proper *teshuvah*. Their *teshuvah* is done out of fear and is performed in haste, not out of true introspection. And so limited is their *teshuvah* that according to the Midrash, only forty years later the city is destroyed because they returned to their evil ways.

So it is difficult to understand this book as an attempt to emphasize the beauty of *teshuvah*. However, precisely because the concept of *teshuvah* is so diminished within this book, it highlights another, more dominant theme. The major theme of this book is not that once people have repented properly and done *teshuvah*, God grants them forgiveness, but rather that *despite the fact that people have not repented, they are still able to receive mercy from God.*

This idea frames the book of Yonah and appears in every single chapter. In chapter 1, God commands Yonah to bring his prophecy of doom to the Ninevites. This command is a total act of mercy because the Ninevites have, so far, done nothing worthy of being saved. In chapter 2, God prepares a fish to swallow Yonah and thus saves Yonah. This too, is a supreme act of mercy because Yonah has not repented and remains obstinate in his rebellion against God. Even in chapter 3, when the Ninevites repent, they do not repent because they expect to be forgiven by God, but only because they hope that they may receive *mercy* from God. They say "*Mi yode'a*" (Who knows), maybe God will turn away from His anger and not destroy us.

Finally, the climax of this work is in chapter 4. Yonah complains to God that his mission to Nineveh was a waste of time, "Because I knew that You were a merciful God [and that You would eventually revoke Your decree]." And then God's piercing reply closes the book: "Should I not then spare the great city of Nineveh with more than a hundred and twenty thousand human beings, who do not know their right hand from their left, and much cattle?"

Perhaps, then, a more accurate explanation for reading this book on Yom Kippur relates to the theme of God's mercy upon all of His creatures. Through the prophecy of Yonah, God is teaching us that His justice and His mercy do not relate to the laws of mankind, whether they are the laws of *teshuvah* or the laws of justice. Rather, God explains that there are no strict rules for mercy, as His infinite ways and His justice elude the comprehension of mere mortals.

God is teaching us that He can and will display His mercy on people who really don't deserve any mercy. God will heal those who don't deserve to be healed; God will save those who don't deserve to be saved. No matter how much you've sinned, God with His infinite wisdom promises that He will display His love and mercy toward you.

And this is why we read the book of Yonah at Minchah on Yom Kippur, just before Ne'ilah. Throughout the Ne'ilah service, the ark remains open as a reminder that the hand of God is always reaching out to us, to uplift those who need extra help in returning. And during Ne'ilah, we praise God, *"Atah noten yad laposhim"* (You stretch out Your hand even to those who are sinners). God never gives up on us. Even when we have stumbled, God reaches out and embraces us.

There is a fundamental difference in our attitudes on Rosh Hashanah and Yom Kippur. On Rosh Hashanah we speak about the obligations of man and society. We reflect on what we must do before God, on what exactly are our responsibilities as human beings. Whereas on Yom Kippur, we beg God to grant us mercy even though we might not deserve His mercy.

This balance between our obligations as servants of God and the mercy of God should reflect itself in the way we approach our relationship with God throughout the year. God is all merciful, but that shouldn't permit us to be lax in our religious responsibilities. We should always motivate ourselves to rise higher in our religious commitment. And on the flip side, our motivation should come from within. The sense of urgency that we feel toward God should not threaten us. We should fear the awesomeness of God, not His threats.

This is a lesson to bear in mind when we struggle to understand and teach Judaism. Our God is all merciful; He is a God Who loves us and all human beings, Who is slow to harm and quick to grant mercy, Who would rather embrace us than chastise us. Our God should be loved more than He should be feared.

Rabbeinu Bachya, a medieval biblical commentator (1255–1340), explains that the harsh sound of the *tekiah* should always be accompanied by the softer sound of the *teruah* precisely in order to teach us this lesson: the sense of urgency before God must always be accompanied by softness and love (Rabbeinu Bachya's commentary to the Torah, Bamidbar 23:21).

And in today's world it is this message of the shofar that should resonate in all our ears. The shofar is a complete sound: the *tekiah* with the *teruah*, our obligations to God and God's merciful love.

Chapter 11
Climbing the Mountain Path

One summer I took some of my children to visit my younger brother Akiva and his family in Portland, Maine, where Akiva then served as a congregational rabbi.

My brother suggested that we visit Peaks Island, a beautiful but tiny island that is accessible only by ferry. According to the 2000 census it is officially home to 843 residents. But as we took the boat over there I wondered just how many of those residents were Jewish.

So we got to the island and went to the bike store to rent bikes and ride around the island on a bike path. I immediately started up a conversation with the owner of the store, Brad, and asked him if he were Jewish. He said, "No, I have a different religion"; but he then proceeded to tell me about a few families living on the island who were Jewish. So I told my brother, "Let's go meet these families and invite them to shul."

At this point, Brad interrupted and said, "What's the matter with me? Don't you want to save my soul?"

So I patiently explained to Brad that it was nothing personal, but he already had a path to travel on. His path, his religion, leads him in one direction. These other Jews on the island have their own path, the Jewish path, and I wanted to see if they need help finding their path. But there can be two paths that go in different directions and still lead us to the same place.

The idea of two different paths leading to the same place is the theme of the Torah reading on the second day of Rosh Hashanah, which tells the story of the Akeidah, or the binding of Yitzchak (Bereishit 22). As Avraham prepares to bind Yitzchak, the phrase that jumps out at us is *"Va'yelkhu sheneihem yachdav"* (And the two of them walked together). This phrase appears not once, but twice. First the Torah says that Avraham took the wood for the offering and placed it on Yitzchak, his son. He took the fire in his hand and the two of them walked together, *"Va'yelkhu sheneihem yachdav."* Rashi explains that the text means that they were walking together even though they had totally different reasons for walking. Avraham who was going to sacrifice his son was walking with *ratzon* and *simchah*, with as much joy and happiness as Yitzchak who did not notice anything unusual.

So they walked together with joy.

But then the text says that Yitzchak asked Avraham, "Where is the lamb for the offering?" And Avraham answered, "God will seek out for Himself the lamb for the offering, my son." And then we are again told, *"Va'yelkhu sheneihem yachdav."* This time Rashi explains the matter differently. Now the phrase *"Va'yelkhu sheneihem yachdav"* means that even though Yitzchak now understood that he was going to be slaughtered, the two of them still walked together toward the mountain with an equal heart – a *lev shaveh*.

Thus, according to Rashi the first time the phrase "they walked together" appears it means that they walked with different intentions on a common path. But the second time it means that they walked with the same mindset on a common path.

There is another possible understanding of the phrase *"Va'yelkhu sheneihem yachdav."* This alternative understanding is core to my approach to Torah and it gives us insight into the repentance process so that we can come closer to Hashem.

The commentators struggle with a simple question: For whom was the Akeidah a bigger test? Was it a bigger test for Yitzchak, since he was prepared to allow himself to be slaughtered? Or was it a bigger test for Avraham, since he was ready and willing to slaughter his own son?

The Izbica Rebbe (Rabbi Mordechai Yosef Leiner, 1801–1854) offers a fascinating perspective on this question. In his work *Mei Hashiloach*, he writes that clearly it was a bigger test for Avraham than for Yitzchak. All Yitzchak had to do was to listen to what his father told him he was supposed to do. On the other hand, Avraham had to listen to God, he had to confirm that God was indeed talking to him, and then he had to understand the proper message from Hashem and finally act in an irreversible way upon that message. That is a much greater test!

But others argue that Yitzchak had the greater test. Rabbi Chayyim ibn Attar (1696–1743) explains in his *Or Hachayyim* commentary on the Torah that this is why God says to Avraham, *"Kach na et binkha"* (*Please* take your son). The *Or Hachayyim* writes that God was telling Avraham to take Yitzchak gently. Avraham had been tested before by God, but Yitzchak was now being tested for the very first time, so Avraham had to take Yitzchak gently, with great care and sensitivity, so as not to overwhelm him with his very first test.

But perhaps the real issue is not who had the greater test, but the fact that they both had great tests. Both tests were real and both tests were great, but the tests were different paths toward Hashem. A challenge of the Akeidah was to see if they would be willing to go together on different paths in life. The Akeidah challenged them to recognize that the other person was facing a different path in life.

This idea that we can have different paths to Hashem is fundamental to my faith. It is one of the main reasons I spoke up passionately against the arrests in 2013 of women who wore prayer shawls (*tallitot*) to the Kotel. These women were associated with a group known as Women of the Wall, which advocates for the rights of women to hold communal prayer services at the Kotel. When members of this group were arrested for carrying a Torah at the Western Wall, I actually criticized Israel publicly.

Please understand how difficult this was for me to do. I love Israel and will defend her to the hilt. But I am deeply afraid that the holiest site of our faith will be turned into an even more exclusive place; I am scared that it will became a place less open to different paths to Hashem. And so I said publicly that we cannot allow the Western Wall to be turned into a Charedi synagogue.

This is the approach to the Akeidah story that is offered by the *Keli Yakar* (Rabbi Shlomo Ephraim Luntschitz, Prague, seventeenth century). The Torah says that when Yitzchak noticed there was no lamb, he turned to his father and said, "*Avi*" (My father). Then he stopped and waited for his father to answer. And Avraham turned to his son and answered, "*Hineni, beni*" (Here I am, my son).

When Yitzchak saw that there was no lamb, all he said was "My father"? The *Keli Yakar* explains that we should read it as a question. Yitzchak wanted to see if Avraham, who was taking him to be slaughtered, was indeed still his father. And so Avraham answered: "Here I am, *my son*." His answer demonstrated that he did in fact still feel toward him as a father to his son. But Avraham continued, "*Elokim yireh Lo haseh l'olah beni*" (God will seek out for Himself the lamb for the offering). "What am I to do?" says Avraham. "I am not the one who chose this path – Hashem did. Hashem chose this difficult path and we must obey."

At that moment, Avraham and Yitzchak understood that Hashem had given each of them different tasks and different tests.

But even though they had different tests, still they had one goal: to serve Hashem. So even though they had different paths they could still walk together, like father and son.

At its core, the Akeidah story is about two people entirely giving of themselves to God and to each other at the same time. Yitzchak could have easily allowed himself to question his father's path and to lash out in anger against it. Avraham could have been dismissive and unforgiving of his son, Yitzchak. But instead we see the opposite. Yitzchak called his father *"avi."* And Avraham said, *"Hineni, beni."* And the two of them walked together with a *lev shaveh*, an equal heart. They recognized that they had different paths to serving Hashem and still they walked together.

This is a critical lesson of the Akeidah. The lesson for our lives is that we can walk together on different paths and remember we are all journeying to the same mountain. That is why I spoke up in support of Women of the Wall. And that is why I told Brad that he has his path and I have my path, but together we are going to the same mountain.

This lesson applies beyond matters of religion. We must understand that people who disagree with us can often be on a different path to the same place.

This message is core to the repentance process. If we want to properly repent, then we need to be able to see the greatness in those who choose a different path than our own. This is the theme of the Rosh Hashanah liturgy: the world is filled with people going down different paths, but when we recognize the greatness in another then we will all walk together to the Temple.

It is often the case that when we see other people challenged with specific tests by God we begin to feel insecure. We might feel insecure about not meeting our specific challenges from God, or we might feel that our own challenges from God are inadequate and don't measure up against this other person's challenges. The message of the Akeidah is that we must walk together even though we have different challenges.

Moreover, a great source of spiritual energy is to recognize that we can each be on different paths, but they lead to the same destination! This recognition will help us to love another and see the greatness in each other.

In chapter 8 ("Mirror Image"), we noted that seeing the greatness of others draws us closer to Hashem. How does this work? What are we supposed to feel when we notice the greatness of others? And what will happen as a result of all this "greatness" that we notice?

The way we envision God is often a metaphor for the way we must engage other people. For example, the rabbis teach us that if we are unwilling to forgive others who have wronged us, then Hashem too, will be unwilling to forgive us for our sins.

The Musaf service of Rosh Hashanah also teaches us this lesson. The structure of this service is not only a reflection of how we envision Hashem, but also of how we must engage with other people.

The Musaf has three sections which are unique to Rosh Hashanah: Malkhiyot, Zikhronot, and Shofarot. Malkhiyot is Kingship. In this section we crown Hashem as King of the universe. In doing so we are declaring that Hashem is great, "*Hashem tzevakot, hu melekh hakavod*" Hashem is Master of the Hosts, He is the King of Honor.

Once we have recognized that God is the great King of the universe, we turn to Zikhronot. We remind God that He loves us. And God remembers "*ahavat kelulotayikh*" (the love of your bridal day; Yirmiyahu 2:2); He recalls his love for us, saying, "*Haven yakir li Efraim?*" – You're my most precious child, Efraim.

Once we acknowledge God's greatness in Malkhiyot, He reciprocates by rekindling His love for us in Zikhronot, which then brings about the third section of Musaf, Shofarot. Shofarot is the blasting of the shofar in recognition that one day soon the whole world will recognize that God is great and all will receive

His love. "And it will be on that day that a great shofar will be blown, and then those lost in Assyria and those cast away in Egypt will come and bow down to Hashem on the holy mountain in Jerusalem."

This three-step process works on an interpersonal level as well. We must recognize the greatness of others – Malkhiyot. This will cause us to love each other – Zikhronot. This will cause us to all walk together on the path to Hashem and blast the shofar on the Temple Mount – Shofarot. The path to our own spiritual greatness comes by first recognizing the greatness of others.

On that same trip to Maine, my children and I decided one day to climb a mountain. As we climbed we noticed that there was a blue trail, a green trail, an orange trail, and a white trail. We decided to take the blue trail. As we ascended the mountain, we felt like we were alone. Since we were the only hikers, we thought it was our own mountain. But when we reached the peak of the mountain we saw many other people, each of whom had taken a different trail to the summit; all the trails reached the same place.

Once we realize that there can be multiple trails to the summit, our own trail will be that much more beautiful and easier to climb.

Chapter 12
Crowning the King

The *Shulchan Arukh* has a chapter entitled "Foods that it is customary to eat on the night of Rosh Hashanah" (*Orach Chayyim* 583). The most famous practice on the night of Rosh Hashanah is to eat a new (and oftentimes exotic) fruit, and an apple and honey. In my family, every year we have a contest about the new fruit to see who can figure out how to eat it. In addition there are other symbolic foods we eat, such as carrots, dates, pomegranates, pumpkins, leeks, beets, the head of a fish, and the head of a lamb.

The traditional reason why we eat these foods is because there is symbolism either in the Hebrew or Yiddish names of these foods or in the foods themselves. Thus, when eating the head of a fish we should say, "May it be Your will, Hashem, that we will be fruitful and multiply like a fish."

In my family we have embraced this practice and our Rosh Hashanah table is bedecked with all of these symbolic and exotic foods. Looking at these foods spread out on the table, I often think that there is another reason for this custom. When the foods are displayed – with all their colors and variety and uniqueness – the table looks like it is fit for a king. This is appropriate for on Rosh Hashanah we are crowning the King of kings.

There are other customs that we practice on Rosh Hashanah to create this festive and intense mood of crowning a king. Thus, the *Shulchan Arukh* records that it is customary to get a haircut on the eve of Rosh Hashanah and to buy a new garment for the holiday.

But of course the most obvious manner in which we create the mood of a coronation ceremony is by blowing the shofar. The shofar is like a trumpet heralding the arrival of a king; when we blow the shofar, we are in effect crowning God as King of the entire world. As the verse we cite in our liturgy declares, "*Bachatzotzrot v'kol shofar hariu lifnei haMelekh, Hashem*" (With trumpets and the sound of the shofar, call out before the King, Hashem; Psalms 98:6).

The basic message of Rosh Hashanah is that we must feel like we are anointing Hashem as King over every aspect of our lives. Rosh Hashanah is about *malkhut*, recognizing the overwhelming dominion of the King. As the *piyyut* of *Hashem Melekh* says, "Hashem is King, Hashem was King, and Hashem will be King forever and ever."

Even though this message of Rosh Hashanah is straightforward, many of us have a hard time internalizing this message. Some of us struggle to really feel that we are in the presence of the King; some of us find it challenging to sense the wonder and excitement that we should feel when crowning a King.

In comparison, I know some people in the United States who woke up in the predawn hours of the day to watch the royal wedding of Prince William to Kate on April 29, 2011. That desire to know the royal doings and the enormous interest in a royal wedding is just an ounce of what we should feel on the holiday of Rosh Hashanah. But, alas, for most of us it is a difficult thing to grasp.

In today's world, it is especially hard to conceive of living with a king in our lives. Just suppose that the president of the United States would call me up and say he wanted to come to shul on Rosh Hashanah. And suppose he placed a condition on his arrival: that we play "Hail to the Chief" with our instruments as he walked up the steps into the synagogue on the holiday. What if I said, "Sure we can. After all, *you're the president!*" Some people might question that decision. And vis-à-vis the president of the United States they would probably be right. But in contrast there is ample precedent to allow such an activity for the sake of a king. A king's honor is so great that we can bend the law out of respect for him due to the legal principle known as *kevod habriot* (respect for human dignity).

The Talmud (*Berakhot* 19b) allowed a *kohen*, who is normally not even allowed to be in the same room as a dead body, to even dance on a coffin in order to give honor to a gentile king who is visiting. Rabbi Meir Simchah of Dvinsk (d. 1922) writes in his classic work *Ohr Sameach* (*Hilkhot Yom Tov* 6:14) about a king who was visiting a nearby town on the second day of *yom tov*. The *Ohr Sameach* permitted the Jewish people to play musical instruments on this second day of *yom tov* as a way of giving honor to the king when he arrived. Incredibly, the rabbinic laws of *yom tov* were suspended for the honor of this king.

If these rulings sound strange to us it is only because we are not used to being in a society that views the king as all powerful. We live in a world in which even the president of the United States is often publically opposed by hecklers and it is entirely legal. Our challenge on Rosh Hashanah is for us to first imagine what it is like to live under a human king of flesh and blood; only then can we begin to contemplate what it is like to live under the King of kings. It is only if we imagine ourselves in the presence of a king that we can understand what it means to crown the true King, the All-Powerful King.

In Rambam's classic fourteen-volume code of law, known as

the *Mishneh Torah*, he concludes the work with an eleven-chapter section called *Hilkhot Melakhim* (Laws of kings). Here are just three laws from that section, which give us insight into the Jewish approach to a human king.

In chapter 2 of *Hilkhot Melakhim*, Rambam writes:

> The king must be treated with great honor. We must implant awe and fear of him in the hearts of all men. The command to "appoint a king" (Devarim17:15) implies the obligation to be in awe of him. We may not ride on his horse, nor sit on his throne, use his scepter, wear his crown, or use any of his utensils. When he dies, they should all be burned before his bier. (2:1)

In chapter 2, law 2, Rambam continues: "No one may ever marry a king's wife." Meaning that even if the king left a widow or if he divorced his wife she would not be permitted to remarry. This was seen as a diminution of the king's greatness. And the following law reads: "It is prohibited to see a king when he is getting a haircut."

We see from here that the Torah gives enormous respect to a king of flesh and blood. But there's a catch – the Torah has an ulterior motive in giving the king such respect. Only through recognizing a king's power can we begin to understand just how much we need to be in awe of Hashem. For as powerful as a king is, whenever we look at him we are reminded that he is not the real King.

The king, too, must demonstrate his complete subservience to Hashem. The proof of this is that a king must carry around a Torah with him at all times to remind himself that he must obey the laws of Hashem. So whenever the people would see the king, they would be reminded that the king serves the ultimate King.

Rosh Hashanah is about helping us to appreciate the *malkhut* of Hashem, our acceptance of God as King over us. When we blow the shofar on Rosh Hashanah we anoint God king and remind ourselves that to be a good Jew means not only to do what God asks us to do, but to do it in a manner that demonstrates that we view Him as the ruler of every aspect of our lives. We must do what He asks simply because He says so; whether or not we understand His ways and whether or not we agree with His commands, we accept them.

But there is a second reason why it is important to understand the nature of a king, and that has to do with why we blow the shofar on Rosh Hashanah.

At first glance, Rambam's *Hilkhot Melakhim* seems irrelevant. After all, we haven't had a king of the Jews for a really long time. Yet not only does Rambam offer eleven chapters about the laws of a king, he does this at a time when the Jewish people were not even a sovereign nation and were living under Islamic and Christian rule. Moreover, he also emphasizes these laws by placing them at the conclusion of the *Mishneh Torah*.

The placement of these laws at the end of Rambam's magnum opus shows both that they are so important and *why* they are so important: as if to say that his fourteen-volume work has as its goal the creation of a king. A true and proper king would theoretically set up a society that totally embodies the values of the Torah; such a society would be the greatest sanctification of God's name.

This is how Rambam ends both *Hilkhot Melakhim* and his entire fourteen-volume *Mishneh Torah*:

> In that era, there will be neither famine nor war, neither envy nor competition, for good will flow in abundance and all the delights will be freely available as dust. The occupation of the entire world will be solely to know God.

The purpose of a human king is to help set up an earthly kingdom for the heavenly King.

But if we have learned anything in history since the time of Rambam, it has been of the great pitfalls of a monarchy. So instead of waiting for a human king, we should take the responsibility upon ourselves as individuals and as communities. This is what the shofar on Rosh Hashanah is reminding us to do – to stay focused with our efforts on one main goal: creating a beautiful Kingdom of God on this earth.

As a verse that we cite in our Rosh Hashanah liturgy states:

> And it will be on that day that a great shofar will be blown and then those lost in Assyria and those cast away in Egypt will come and bow down to Hashem on the holy mountain in Jerusalem. (Yeshayahu 27:13)

This verse about the shofar is not referring to this year's Rosh Hashanah, when we, as it were, place a crown on Hashem's head. Instead, it is a prayer and a prophecy: just like we are crowning Him this Rosh Hashanah, so one day in the future the entire world will also crown Him as King. But we will only get there if we first accept God as our King; then we can work to make the entire world a reflection of God.

Firstly, we need to accept God as our King Whom we must obey at all times, whether or not we understand or like what He says. Secondly, we must always be working to perfect His kingdom. That is what the shofar of Rosh Hashanah is all about: it is a reminder of who we are and what we are trying to accomplish.

When we hear the shofar, let us realize that we are crowning God King. Let us imagine what that really means and let us commit ourselves to be His soldiers and create His kingdom.

Chapter 13
How to Keep a New Year's Resolution

A fundamental aspect of Rosh Hashanah is that of *teshuvah*, or repentance. As part of the *teshuvah* process one must make a specific confession known as *vidui*. The great Rambam records the text of the confession for us:

> How does one confess? He states: "I implore You, God, I sinned, I transgressed, I committed iniquity before You by doing the following. Behold, I regret and am embarrassed by my actions. *And I promise never to repeat this act again* [*U'leolam eini chozer l'davar zeh*]. (*Mishneh Torah, Hilkhot Teshuvah* 1:2)

I promise never to repeat this act again.
Is that really a smart thing to do? To make a promise on the *Yamim Noraim* that there is a pretty good chance we won't be able to keep…. After all, don't we all go back to our same old mistakes once we leave the spiritual glow of the High Holidays?

A 2007 study by Richard Wiseman from the University of Bristol involving three thousand people showed that *88 percent of those who set New Year resolutions fail,* despite the fact that 52 percent of the study's participants were confident of success at the beginning. (See Richard Wiseman, "New Year's Resolutions Experiments," http://www.quirkology.com/UK/Experiment_resolution.shtml; and Jonah Lehrer, "Blame It on the Brain," *Wall Street Journal,* December 26, 2009.)

But it doesn't have to be that way. We can improve our chances of success in our New Year's resolutions. The story of Chanah and Shmuel, which we read as the haftarah for the first day of Rosh Hashanah, can serve as a paradigm for us to follow. Chanah and Shmuel are both models of people who made resolutions and completely followed through on their resolutions. There are many reasons why we read the story of Chanah and Shmuel on the first day of Rosh Hashanah; one reason is that this story is an example not only of how God keeps His commitment to us, but also of how people should and do keep their commitments to God.

When Chanah is crying out to Hashem and praying for a child, the verse tells us:

> And she vowed a vow, and said: "O Hashem Tzevakot, if you will notice the pain of Your servant, and remember me, and not forget Your servant, but will give to Your servant a seed among men, then I will dedicate him to You for all the days of his life, and a razor shall not come upon his head." (I Samuel 1:11)

The book of Shmuel makes clear that Chanah keeps her vow and dedicates Shmuel in service to Hashem for his whole life. The Bible states that Chanah declares: *"Hu shaul laHashem"* (He is lent to Hashem; 1 Samuel 1:28). The Talmud (*Nazir* 66a) tells us that according to Rabbi Nehorai, Shmuel was a *nazir* forever; i.e., not only did Chanah keep her resolution while she was alive, but even after her death Shmuel remained dedicated to Hashem for his entire life. He kept her resolution even after she died.

Our job on Rosh Hashanah is to learn from Chanah and Shmuel how to keep our own resolutions, not just till the end of Rosh Hashanah but for the rest of our lives. So what is the key to walking in the footsteps of Chanah and making our resolutions successful?

There are three steps to making a successful resolution.

Step One

Make a resolution that you can succeed in. You will have greater chance of success if you make a *limited and concrete resolution.*

That same study from the University of Bristol notes that men achieved their goal 22 percent more often when they engaged in goal setting – a system in which small, measurable goals are being set, such as a pound a week, instead of the more general goal of losing weight.

The Talmud tells us that Shmuel was a *nazir* for his whole life. The source for this is that Chanah said in her prayer to God, "A razor will not come on his head." A *nazir* is someone who takes an oath to prohibit himself from coming into contact with a dead body, drinking wine or a grape product, and taking a haircut.

A *nazir* is the paradigm in Jewish life of someone who commits himself entirely to God. It is the closest thing that Judaism has to a monk. But it is significant, when put in that context, that a *nazir* is really a very limited commitment. All a *nazir* does is limit three things: contact with the dead, drinking wine, and cutting hair. In the scheme of things this is a limited and realistic commitment. Notice that Chanah promises to dedicate her son to God but then the text immediately qualifies it by saying that this dedication simply means that "a razor will not come upon his head." The lesson is that we should make a resolution that is meaningful and impactful, yet limited in scope.

Think about a specific, limited resolution that you can take upon yourself for the coming year. Think about how you can apply it in a concrete manner. For example, you might say you are going to be careful not to gossip for one hour a day, or increase your Torah study by one hour a week, or call your loved ones every single day.

Step Two

When making a resolution and following through on that resolution, don't expect immediate gratification.

Let's take physical exercise as an example. Someone might make a resolution to exercise every day for half an hour. The first week of exercise the person might love it and it will feel great, but then after a while it will get boring and the person might quit exercising. That's why how we feel when performing the resolution is irrelevant; we should not focus on it. We should focus on why we are exercising, not how we feel when we exercise. Thus, for example, we should exercise because it makes us healthier people and not because we feel good when exercising.

Or let's say we take it upon ourselves to go to Friday night services every week. The first week we might love the service. We might love that the tunes are upbeat and the service uplifting. But then, after a while, we might get bored and say, "Oh, the service is not as enjoyable as it once was." And then, once our pleasure decreases, we might stop going. That would be a mistake. Instead we should say, "I am going to go to Friday night services because that is what I believe God wants me to do. If it feels good, great; if not, then I will work on myself to try and get a better spiritual result from the service."

The key is to never let our personal feelings of pleasure interfere with our commitments to our resolutions.

This too, is a lesson we learn from the story of Chanah and Shmuel. Shmuel was a Levite and he was a descendant of the wicked biblical figure Korach. Korach was so wicked that he took on Moshe Rabbeinu in a fight. Moshe was such a giant; how could Korach think he was greater than Moshe?

Rashi tells us:

> But what did Korach, who was astute, see [to commit] this folly? His vision deceived him. He saw [prophetically] that a chain of great people descended from him: Shmuel, who is equal [in importance] to Moshe and Aharon. (Rashi, Bamidbar 16:7)

Korach looked into the future and saw that Shmuel was his descendant. Given Shmuel's greatness, Korach figured that as his ancestor, he too must be correct in his battle with Moshe. Korach assumed that his descendant Shmuel got his natural ability from him.

But Korach was all wrong. He was from the tribe of Levi, and so was the father of Shmuel, Elkanah, but if it were up to these two people then there never would have been a Shmuel Hanavi. Shmuel came into existence because of the commitment and dedication of his mother Chanah.

It was Chanah who did not take no for an answer from God. It was Chanah who showed tremendous perseverance in her dream of having a child. Elkanah said to Chanah, "Am I not better for you than ten sons?" (1 Shmuel 1:8). It was as if Elkanah were saying to Chanah, "Don't I make you feel good?"

And maybe Elkanah was "better" for Chanah than ten sons. But the point that Chanah taught was that it is not about what feels "better" at any single moment, but about what our goals are. Her goal was to have a child who would be totally dedicated to Hashem. Since her goal was to have a child, she didn't settle for what made her feel good, and she didn't settle for merely having a child. She put her heart and soul into her goal. As the story tells us, Chanah would make her son Shmuel a robe and bring it up with her every year when she came to serve God (ibid. 2:19). She was consistent and focused.

Korach and Elkanah might have had great natural ability, but they would have both failed to produce a child as great as Shmuel Hanavi because they had the wrong approach. Their approach was focused on their own personal satisfaction and thus dulled their commitment to the ultimate goal of serving God. It was Chanah who had the focus and the commitment that birthed Shmuel.

Step Three

Never doubt your own ability to be successful.

Many of us fail in our goals because we think we just can't do it. We think it is beyond us. We give up. Chanah succeeded because she realized that God put her in this world in order to excel. We are God's creatures and since God is great, we who are created in His image must also be great.

Chanah turned to God and said:

> Master of the universe, there is nothing extraneous in anything You created.... Eyes to see, ears to hear, a nose to smell, a mouth to speak, hands for work, legs to walk, breasts to nurse. These breasts that You placed upon my heart, should I not nurse with them? Give me a son and I will nurse with them. (*Berakhot* 31b)

Just like Chanah felt that she was created for a reason, we were all created for a reason. We should never give up on our dreams or set our sights low. Rosh Hashanah is a reminder that we are great and we have the ability to succeed. Do we want to diet or quit smoking? No problem. God created us, so we can do it. Do we want to control our temper or our tendency to gossip? God created us with the ability to do it.

In sum, there are three steps to help make our resolutions successful: 1) make a specific and limited resolution; 2) don't confuse momentary enjoyment with the goal of the resolution; and 3) don't ever doubt your ability to follow through and successfully complete the resolution.

We often think of *teshuvah* simply as improving ourselves, becoming better people. But maybe we need to think of it as a series of making and keeping concrete promises. And if we make those promises to our friends, then we are even better off.

Here is a bonus hint: *Resolutions are more likely to succeed when they are publicly shared and when there is support from friends.*

I know this is true because a few years ago I shared with our congregation that I would start exercising on a regular basis. There have been times since then that I have lost the desire to fulfill my commitment, but because of my public stance on it I have been true to my commitment.

Every year before Rosh Hashanah we should bear this in mind as we spiritually prepare for the holiday. We should seek out a resolution for the coming year and share it communally with our friends and family. This will give us a better chance of beating the odds and keeping our commitments. It will also remind us that we are all in this together!

Chapter 14
Rekindling Our Romance with God

The longest marriage listed in the *Guinness Book of World Records* is the marriage between Herbert and Zelmyra Fisher. They lived in James City, North Carolina, and were married for eighty-six years. They got married on May 13, 1924, and lived together happily until Mr. Fisher passed away on February 27, 2011, at the age of 105. Zelmyra was 103 years old at the time of her husband's death. No, they weren't Jewish. In reading up about them, one of the facts I found fascinating was that throughout their lives they kept separate memberships at two different churches, which they each separately attended every week.

By all accounts they had a very happy marriage. Thank God for that, because eighty-six years would be a long time to live in an unhappy marriage.

While Herbert and Zelmyra were married for eighty-six years, the truth is that I know of another marriage that has lasted even longer than theirs. This marriage has not been entirely good. There have been ups and downs. But it is a beautiful marriage and a great story. I am talking about the marriage of God to the Jewish people.

The marriage of God to the Jewish people goes back to Mount Sinai, which our rabbis say was like a wedding between God and the Jewish people (see Rashi, Shemot 31:18). One of the messages of Rosh Hashanah is that we should always remember that just like God loved us at Sinai, He still loves us today.

The haftarah that we read on the second day of Rosh Hashanah comes from Yirmiyahu, chapter 31 (1–20). At a time when the Jewish people were feeling rejected and forgotten, Yirmiyahu conveys the following message:

> From afar Hashem appears to me, saying: "I have loved you with an eternal love [*ahavat olam ahavtikh*]; therefore I have extended kindness to you." (Yirmiyahu 31:2)

Right when we are feeling the most rejected – at the time of our first exile from the land of Israel – God appeared to our prophet, Yirmiyahu. God was far away from us. We might have thought that our relationship with Him was over forever. But instead He reminded us that He loved us once and the He will love us forever.

But in order to fully appreciate God's love, we must love Him back with all our hearts. In the Zikhronot section of the Rosh Hashanah Musaf we recite the verse from Yirmiyahu (2:2) in which Hashem tells us, "*Zakharti lakh chesed ne'urayikh*" – I remember for your sake the kindness of your youth, the love of your bridal days, how you followed Me through the wilderness in an unsown land. We once had a romantic relationship with God, and on Rosh Hashanah we are trying to rekindle that relationship. We are retelling the story of our relationship by talking about how we were once so in love with God that we followed Him through a barren wilderness. It is like a married couple who have grown distant over the years. Somehow, they lost their spark. But then they find their wedding video and turn it on. Suddenly all the romance and love comes flooding back into their lives.

The goal of Rosh Hashanah is to reestablish our loving, and romantic, relationship with God.

Rambam ends his *Hilkhot Teshuvah* with the following *halakhah*:

> A person should love God with a very great and exceeding love until his soul is bound up in the love of God. Thus, he will always be obsessed with this love as if he is lovesick.
>
> [A lovesick person's] thoughts are never diverted from the love of that woman. He is always obsessed with her – when he sits down, when he gets up, when he eats and drinks. With an even greater [love], the love for God should be [implanted] in the hearts of those who love Him and are obsessed with Him at all times as we are commanded, "[Love God] with all your heart and with all soul" (Devarim 6:5). (*Mishneh Torah, Hilkhot Teshuvah* 10:3)

Thus, one goal of the High Holidays is to remind us to love God with all of our hearts and for us as a people, as communities, and as individuals, to rekindle the romantic relationship we once had with Him.

A *message* of Rosh Hashanah is that God loves us forever. No matter how far we have gone away from Him, He still loves us and we can still return to Him. And the *goal* of Rosh Hashanah is for us to do *teshuvah*, to return to Him, and rekindle our love of God. But how do we accomplish our goal? How do we rekindle our loving relationship with God?

As in any loving relationship, there are ups and downs. Good times and tough times. So too, in our relationship with God, we have our ups and downs. Rosh Hashanah is supposed to inspire us to get back to a great place in that relationship.

I would like to offer three suggestions as to how we can accomplish our goal of rekindling our love affair with God.

Suggestion No. 1

Remember back to when you had a great moment with God.

Think back to a special moment in your life when you felt closely connected to Hashem. Maybe it was on your first visit to Israel. Or maybe it was the first time you kept Shabbat. For me, it was the moment when I saw my child being born. I have never been closer to God then when I witnessed the miracle of a human life being created.

Take a moment and visualize that *"aha"* moment in your life. Think about how awesome you felt at that moment. That is a moment of pure bliss that we want to hold on to. It is such an amazing feeling. When we feel bliss like that we are reaping the benefits of a relationship with Hashem.

We will rekindle our loving relationship with God if we remember those great moments. I believe that those moments of pure spirituality are the actual rewards that the prophet promises us that we will receive for serving Hashem.

Yirmiyahu tells us in the haftarah that Hashem loves us so much that we will get immediate benefit from keeping His mitzvot. This is what Yirmiyahu tells us will happen to us if we love Hashem:

> They shall stream to Hashem's goodness, by the grain, by the wine, and by the oil, and by the young sheep and cattle; then their soul shall be like a well-watered garden, and they shall no more agonize. Then the maiden shall rejoice in the dance, and the young boys and old men shall join together; I shall transform their mourning to joy and I shall comfort them and gladden them in place of their grief. (Yirmiyahu 31:11–12)

Yirmiyahu tells us that if we have a relationship with Hashem, He will nourish every aspect of our life. This is one of the greatest kindnesses that God does for us. He not only tells us that we must keep the mitzvot but He also makes it easy for us because keeping the mitzvot is such a joy and it brings us so much pleasure and sustenance in our daily lives. These are the benefits of being spiritual and religious.

This is what Hashem promises us in the haftarah. "*Yesh sakhar li'feulatekh*" (There is a reward for your accomplishments). These are the benefits of religion: if we follow Hashem's way, then we will bask in the joy and the glory of His presence. It is a reward very much based in this world, and how much more so in the future world.

So that is the first suggestion about how we can increase our love of God. We should think about how great it is to have a relationship with Hashem; we should contemplate all the pleasures and nourishment we get from Him. The more we think about it, the more we will appreciate what He gives us and the more we will run to His embrace.

Thus, the first suggestion is to *remember what brought us here in the first place*.

Suggestion No. 2
Actively nurture your relationship with Hashem.

We can actively nurture our relationship with Hashem by telling the story of how we once had a beautiful relationship with God. The telling of this story reminds us of what we once had, and hopefully it will awaken our hearts and inspire us to once again recapture that moment.

As a practical suggestion, one way we can "tell the story" and sustain our relationship with God throughout the year is through Torah study. There are many different ways to accomplish this but I suggest studying the stories of Tanakh. The more we study our Bible the more we are telling the story of our historical relationship with God and the greater our understanding of what we once had. More knowledge leads to more love.

For me personally, one of the greatest pleasures I have in my life is just reading and rereading the weekly Torah portion with Rashi. It tells us the story of our people in a beautiful and charming way. This is not just a nice practice; it is also a requirement of Jewish law. Jewish law requires everyone to read the portion of the week twice, with the commentary of Targum. Some suggest that Rashi is the equivalent to the Targum. One special moment for me was when I spoke at my third grader's Rashi party. The message I shared with them was what my third-grade rebbe told me: "Rashi is my best friend. And I bless you that Rashi also become your best friend." Every week I open up Rashi on the *chumash* and he tells me what to think and how to feel. I see my notes from last year on the side of the page and I remember what he taught me in the past. For me, reading Rashi inspires me every week to come closer to Hashem.

Another source of great comfort for me is the daily study of the Talmud as part of the Daf Yomi. Every day I open the pages of the Talmud and feel a connection to God as I continue a conversation with generations of our ancestors.

If you are seeking to nurture a relationship with Hashem then one recommendation I have is to commit to a daily study of either Tanakh, Rashi, or the Daf Yomi.

Suggestion No. 3

The third suggestion as to how we can increase our love of God requires more of us. The Mishnah says, *"Lefum tzaara agra"* (According to the effort is the reward; Avot 5:23). Thus, *if we want God to commit to us then we need to recommit to Him.*

God tells us in the haftarah that He loves us forever. But it's not so simple, as anyone who has ever been married knows – marriage can be the most amazing thing in the world, but in all love affairs there can be moments that run the full gamut of emotions.

So too, God also tells us that the path to Him is not easy. As part of our searching for God, Yirmiyahu tells us that there will be days when the path will be rocky and hard going. When we finally get to Him it will literally be as a result of blood, sweat, and tears. "*Bi'vkhi yavo'u*" (With weeping they will come; Yirmiyahu 31:8). With weeping we will come to God...

I just spoke about the greatness of God for making religion so enjoyable. So why is Yirmiyahu telling us that we will come to God weeping? What does this weeping mean?

The weeping is not the weeping of pain or of sadness, but the weeping of soul-searching. Rabbi Joseph Soloveitchik writes that when the Jews will return to Hashem they will "then see their nation in a completely new light and they will burst out in tears" (*Rosh Hashanah Machzor, with commentary adapted from the teachings of Rabbi Joseph B. Soloveitchik*, comp. and ed. Dr. Arnold Lustiger [New York: Kahl and OU Press, 2007], 425).

The weeping represents a serious effort on our behalf to think about our commitment to Hashem and to act on it. Only when we do that can we approach Him and feel His love. God gives us the opportunity to feel Him. It is a gift of God, but if we want to get any of the rewards that God promises us then we need to put our heart and soul into God as well.

Sometimes people tell me, "I want to do more religiously but I just can't give any more time to it. My work needs me, my spouse needs me, my children need me." I always nod my head. I don't want to argue with people. But I think it is my duty to say that I also think that the more people commit their time to God the better spouses they will be and the better parents and children they will be.

I have come full circle on this. When I was in college and they were talking to us about the best way to encounter the unaffiliated, the message we heard is don't say, "*Schwer zu sein ein yid*" (It's hard to be a Jew). They told me that doesn't work anymore; instead we should say, "It's fun to be a Jew." I fundamentally agree with that: it is great and it is fun to be a Jew.

But the pendulum has also swung a little too much. Now we

hear so much about how great it is to be a Jew, but what about how hard it is to be a Jew? How being a Jew requires tremendous commitment to Hashem. If being Jewish is just about being fun, then we will never reach our full potential. We have to commit to Hashem if we really want to love Him. Can you imagine being in a loving relationship without committing? I can't and I wouldn't want it.

Hashem will always love us and He will always keep the door open for us to love Him back. *Teshuvah* means figuring out how we can love Hashem. My suggestions are that we can do a better job of loving Hashem if we retell His story which is also our story, if we recognize that there is a "reward for our efforts," and if we commit to Him the way He commits to us.

Chapter 15
Striving for Spiritual Honesty

On Rosh Hashanah we stand before God and we say, "*Mi yichyeh u'mi yamut*" (Who will live and who will die). It is a holiday on which the mortality of our lives is thrust in our faces over and over again. In this context, it is appropriate to remind everyone of a question that the Talmud discusses: What will be the first question that the heavenly court asks us when we go up to heaven?

There are two different answers to this question. For now we will only discuss the answer offered in tractate *Shabbat* (31a). The Talmud explains that after we die the very first thing we will be asked is, "*Nasata v'natata b'emunah?*" (Did you engage in business properly?).

This is the first issue Hashem will ask us about? Were we honest? Did we carry ourselves with integrity? This teaches us just how vital it is for a spiritual person to live a life of honesty.

I want to tell you a story about my grandfather and honesty.

My grandfather came to Belgium as a poor refugee from Warsaw. He had a very hard time making a living and breaking into the business community. On the day my father was born my grandfather went for a walk in the park, anxious about how he was going to support his family. He sat down on a park bench and stuck his hand under the bench, only to find a bag of diamonds. He could have kept those diamonds, which had no recognizable sign on them. Instead he tracked down the owner and returned the diamonds. That man became his good friend and helped him find a job as a diamond cutter. Later, when the Nazis came and were threatening my grandfather and my father's whole family, this man – the owner of the diamonds – arranged for my father's family to escape. Were it not for my grandfather's pure honesty, I would not be here today.

But of course, the reason to be honest is not because it might help us out one day. The reason to be honest is because without honesty we are nothing; without integrity we are living a lie.

One of the areas that is most important to me in my rabbinate is that my community and my shul be associated with integrity and honesty. I try very hard to make this a focus of my rabbinate. It pains me deeply when I read about examples of otherwise Torah-observant Jews, and especially rabbis, who commit dishonest acts and act without integrity. When I read of such things I am horrified and I often feel the need to speak out. Not because I want to hurt the person even more, but because we need to make clear that such behavior is the opposite of the path of Torah.

Some people take the approach that it is better to not talk about such *shandehs* (scandals). Better to be quiet and focus on the good. But we can't do that. Firstly, in today's world, it is harder to keep these things a secret. The stories come out and if we don't denounce them forcefully then it appears that we are agreeing with them. And secondly, and even more importantly, some people will read about these scandals and shrug their shoulders and say, "Who needs religion." Some people will get turned off spiritually when they read about a lack of integrity in the Jewish community.

We have to take a different approach to such scandals. We have to take a spiritual approach that will allow us to react to such news in a way that will bring us closer to Hashem. There is a deep lesson here that is core to our spirituality and core to what our Rosh Hashanah needs to be about.

There is a phrase that we would do well to keep in mind on Rosh Hashanah. We should make this phrase the mantra of our *Yamim Noraim*: *"Ein kategor ne'esah sanegor"* (A prosecutor doesn't become a defense attorney). This phrase symbolizes what it means to be a Jew, especially during the holidays. Let's explore what it means and why it is so core to our spirituality.

The Talmud uses this phrase, *Ein kategor ne'esah sanegor*, in connection with a law about a shofar. The Mishnah (*Rosh Hashanah* 26a) states: *"Kol hashofarot kesherim chutz mi'shel parah mipnei she'hu keren"* – horns of all animals are fit to be used for the mitzvah of blowing the shofar on Rosh Hashanah except for the horn of a cow, since the horn of a cow is not called a shofar but a *keren*.

The Talmud wonders about this reason for the disqualification of a cow's horn, since other horns are also sometimes called *keren*. For this reason, the Talmud offers a second explanation for the disqualification of a cow's horn. The Talmud says that we don't use a cow's horn on Rosh Hashanah for the same reason that the *kohen gadol* did not wear his normal garments of gold when he entered the Holy of Holies on Yom Kippur. The reason is that *ein kategor ne'esah sanegor*.

The phrase literally means that we cannot permit the prosecutor to serve as the defense. Rashi (ad locum) explains that the gold garments of the *kohen gadol* are a reminder of the sin of the golden calf. Every day the *kohen gadol* wears eight special garments, some of which contain gold. But when he performs the service in the Holy of Holies on Yom Kippur he needs to remove his golden garments and put on garments of pure white. The reason is that on Yom Kippur he is especially trying to atone for the sin of the golden calf – the greatest sin in Jewish history – and it would be inconsistent to wear the golden garments into the Holy of Holies. It would be like if a person were caught on video camera stealing a suit from a store, and then when that person came before the judge for sentencing – and to beg for leniency – he showed up wearing the exact same suit! He would never do that, for *ein kategor ne'esah sanegor*. So too, if we sounded the horn of a cow on Rosh Hashanah it would be another reminder of the sin of the golden calf. We can't do that – *ein kategor ne'esah sanegor*.

I will always remember the first time I heard this phrase. I was sitting in shul next to my father and he leaned over and explained to me that the *kohen gadol* wears white on Yom Kippur because of *ein kategor ne'esah sanegor*. As a young boy, I thought it was a funny phrase, with its strange-sounding words and rhymes.

But it is not just a cute teaching. It is of major significance. Some argue (see *Encyclopedia Talmudit*, 1:602, s.v. *ein kategor*) that this is an actual biblical law since it is the reason that the *kohen gadol* wears only white garments in his special Yom Kippur service.

As well, we have actual *halakhot* and practical ramifications based upon the concept of *ein kategor ne'esah sanegor*. It was taught in the name of the great medieval pietist, Rabbi Yehudah Hechasid, that if one bought a book that had originally been written with less than pure intentions then one is not permitted to use this book for a holy purpose. And so the halakhists debate the question as to whether or not we can use a prayer book that was printed on Shabbat. The reason why it is problematic is because *ein kategor ne'esah sanegor*. (See Hagahot Maimoniot to *Avodah Zarah* 7:2.)

Also, because of *ein kategor ne'esah sanegor* a person who is a "*baal machloket*" – a rabble-rouser – should not be appointed to blow the shofar or be the *chazzan* on Rosh Hashanah. The High

Holidays are a time of unity and peace and it is a contradiction to that message to have a leader who represents the opposite of that (*Encyclopedia Talmudit*, ibid.).

One last example: Rabbi Akiva Eger (1761–1837, *Orach Chayyim* 610:4) rules that one should not wear any gold at all on Yom Kippur because of the principle of *ein kategor ne'esah sanegor*. Previously we saw that the *kohen gadol* did not wear gold when he served in the Holy of Holies, but Rabbi Akiva Eger is teaching us that many people took upon themselves the spirit of this law in their own practice and behavior. These people felt that it would be inconsistent with Yom Kippur, a day where we beg forgiveness for so many sins, to wear gold. (However, he does remind us that this law only applies to men and not women, since women did not participate in the sin of the golden calf.)

Thus, this idea of *ein kategor* figures prominently in the High Holidays. It dictates what the *kohen gadol* wears and what kind of shofar we blow. It tells us what we can wear to shul, which prayer books we can use, and who can be our *chazzan*. The point, however, is not simply for us to refrain from wearing gold on Yom Kippur. The real point is for us to understand the significance of this phrase and why it is such an important part of the High Holidays.

The *Yamim Noraim* are about *teshuvah*. *Teshuvah* literally means repentance, but it implies spiritual self-awareness and spiritual improvement.

The most important part of *teshuvah* is being honest with ourselves. The *teshuvah* confession recorded by Rambam contains the words "*harei nichamti u'voshti b'maasai*" (behold I regret and am embarrassed by my actions; *Mishneh Torah, Hilkhot Teshuvah* 1:2). Rambam tells us that whoever does *teshuvah* in a dishonest manner is doing a worthless *teshuvah*. Rambam also tells us: "One who says, 'I will sin and then repent' – such a person is unable to do *teshuvah*" (ibid. 4:1). Similarly, Rambam writes that people who confess with their words but do not really mean it – the repentance is worthless (ibid. 2:4).

The basic message of *teshuvah* is that if we are not honest our repentance is pointless. This is what *ein kategor ne'esah sanegor* means. Our actions must be suffused with honesty and integrity. Our actions must reflect a drive for spiritual consistency – consistency between what we say in our prayers and what we do with our actions. It is not OK to lie, cheat, steal, and hurt people, and then make it all better by reciting prayers with extra fervor or writing a brilliant article or delivering an inspiring lecture.

This is especially true when we stand before God on Rosh Hashanah and beg to come into His presence. On Rosh Hashanah, the principle of *ein kategor ne'esah sanegor* reminds us to strive for spiritual consistency and integrity. If we don't strive for consistency with what we preach and what we do, and if we are not spiritually honest, then we cannot hope to achieve spiritual success.

As we grow in our Jewish life we will of course be inconsistent. One day we'll pray with intensity, the other day we might even forget a blessing. But through our growth, integrity and honesty always need to be the prerequisite to spirituality.

What does it mean to be spiritually honest? It can mean a lot of things, but we can start by focusing on five things:

1. A prerequisite for a quality prayer is commitment to proper moral behavior.

2. Immoral behavior is endemic in our society, but we have to hold ourselves to a higher standard. The Torah teaches us that we have a special responsibility to be different and to be a light unto the nations.

3. When we hear of scandals involving Torah scholars a spiritual reaction would be for us to remind ourselves to be different. We won't be like them. We will be better. We will be even more honest, even less hypocritical. The shortcomings we see in others will inspire us to aim higher for ourselves.

4. When we choose our spiritual leaders we will honor them for their values and the way they live their lives. This should be even more important than how brilliant they are.

5. Before we begin our own prayers on Rosh Hashanah and Yom Kippur, before we even utter one word, we should think about this and contemplate whether we are living a life of integrity. How can we do even better? How can we improve? Without honesty, our spirituality is bankrupt.

Even though we should always strive for a life of spiritual honesty, there is a special emphasis in this area when we come to the High Holidays. On the High Holidays we are supposed to bare our souls before God. We are supposed to take advantage of the special power of the time in order to connect to Hashem. If we lose this opportunity it is doubly sad.

The Talmud explains that when we blow the shofar the moment is so powerful that it is comparable to when the *kohen gadol* entered the Holy of Holies on Yom Kippur. The Talmud (*Rosh Hashanah* 26a) states that even though the shofar is blown outside of the Holy of Holies, it is comparable to the Holy of Holies because the shofar is a type of offering to God, as holy as when the *kohen gadol* made his offering in the Holy of Holies. In the words of Ritva (ad. loc.), it is like a pleasing sacrifice before Hashem (*"lehitratzot el adonav"*).

When we blow the shofar we have the opportunity to be standing before Hashem. When we blow the shofar we have the opportunity to ask ourselves one simple question that pervades every aspect of our lives: Are we living our lives with honesty? And if not, God forbid, how can we improve in this area?

There is a story told about Reb Levi Yitzchak of Berditchev. One year he was interviewing candidates to be the shofar blower for his congregation. He asked each one: "What will be your *kavvanah* when you sound the shofar? One said that he would use the *kavvanot* found in kabbalah, another said that he would focus on the ten meanings of the shofar found in the writings of Rav Saadyah Gaon, and the others all gave similar answers. He kept rejecting all the candidates. Finally, one candidate explained that he was not a scholar. He admitted that when he would go to sleep at night he worried about being able to marry off his four daughters. So before he would blow the shofar he wanted to say a special silent prayer for Hashem to listen to the sound of his shofar and help him provide for his daughters. Reb Levi Yitzchak chose this man to blow the shofar for the congregation because of his honesty (see Samuel H. Dresner, *Levi Yitzhak of Berditchev: Portrait of a Hasidic Master* [Hartmore House, 1974]). Without plain honesty all the erudition in the world is meaningless.

Rosh Hashanah is about spiritual honesty – this is what *ein kategor ne'esah sanegor* means. It means that we can't be hypocritical. But beyond that, it is about always pushing ourselves in the area of integrity, always striving for more. When we walk before Hashem we must walk with integrity and strive for spiritual honesty.

Chapter 16
Working toward a Communal Prayer

Rosh Hashanah is a time to focus on the power and the pitfalls of communal prayer – about what we should strive for when we pray as a community, and what should be the focus of our communal concerns. We spend a large part of our time in synagogue listening to the *chazzan* chant the repetition of the Amidah – the *chazarat hashatz*.

The source for *chazarat hashatz* is actually based upon the laws learned from the blowing of the shofar on Rosh Hashanah. The last Mishnah in tractate *Rosh Hashanah* teaches: "Every individual is obligated to blow the shofar on Rosh Hashanah." There is an obligation on every person to blast the shofar (or hear it blasted) on Rosh Hashanah. The great sage, Rabban Gamliel, adds to this position. He teaches that the representative of the community blasts the shofar and thus fulfills the obligation on behalf of everyone else.

My interpretation of this Mishnah (and there are different ways to read it) is that Rabban Gamliel is adding to the position of the *tanna kamma*, the anonymous author of the Mishnah. The author of the Mishnah puts forward the position that it is preferable that people blast the shofar for themselves. Rabban Gamliel then states that in addition, one person – the leader – should blast the shofar on behalf of everyone.

Rabban Gamliel's position seems to be that when praying to God, the ideal is that the entire community should also be represented with one sound. Prayer should go up separately from individuals, and also as a complete unit on behalf of the entire community.

The shofar is a trumpet sound, but it is also a prayer. It is the purest prayer that goes directly to God. The way we blow shofar today, it is also a communal prayer. One person blows the shofar as a prayer on behalf of the community.

When it comes to our prayers today, we follow both suggestions of the Mishnah. We have individual and communal prayers. We pray a silent Amidah, which represents our individual prayers. And through the leader of the congregation we repeat the Amidah.

The source for this repetition of the Amidah is Rabban Gamliel's teaching. Just like Rabban Gamliel counseled that one person should blast the shofar on behalf of everyone, so too, he believed that one person should recite the words of the Amidah aloud on behalf of everyone.

When the shofar is blown, the entire congregation is focused on it. That is the paradigm of communal prayer. So too, the *chazarat hashatz* should be seen as a communal Amidah. Just as the shofar is blasted by one and intended for all, so too the communal Amidah is said by one and intended for all.

Therefore, when we hear the repetition of the Amidah, it is a time to focus on prayers on behalf of the community. It's a time to think of communal needs. Every community has challenges and concerns. During the silent Amidah we pray for our own thoughts; during the repetition we shift gears and focus on the needs of the community.

There is also something else occurring during the *chazarat hashatz*. There is a comment upon Rabban Gamliel's position found in the Talmud that states: "The people in the fields who were busy working and unable to come to pray, fulfilled their obligations for prayer through the communal Amidah" (*Rosh Hashanah* 35a). They fulfilled their obligation to pray even though they did not hear the communal prayer at all! How is this possible? How could the people in the fields who were unable to pray fulfill their obligation of prayer?

In this *halakhah* is contained the power of communal prayer. When a community gathers and prays together, then the power of their prayers spread far and wide. When a community focuses on the communal Amidah and treats it with the same respect that they treat their own personal Amidah, then it affects not only those in their own minyan, but also those in the wider world.

When the communal Amidah is done properly, it represents a sensitivity and concern for the larger community. It symbolizes a caring for those beyond our own immediate four walls. It speaks of a yearning for a connection with people throughout the world. This is why the people in the fields can fulfill their obligation without doing anything. The powerful communal Amidah has reached them.

So the communal Amidah carries with it two potent messages. Like the blast of the shofar, it represents the desire to offer one united prayer to God. And it seeks to connect with those throughout the world who might not know how to pray.

Chapter 17
The Sounds of the Shofar against the Backdrop of War

After the Abrabanel synagogue was attacked by an angry mob of anti-Semites in the heart of Paris in July 2014, I traveled in solidarity with Rabbi Etan Mintz to visit the synagogue and to lend my support. I was honored to be invited to give the devar Torah to the synagogue on Shabbat and I was fortunate enough to build a lasting and meaningful friendship with the community.

What I saw there scared me. I saw a beautiful synagogue in the year 2014 attacked by a mob in perhaps the most sophisticated city in the world. This realization shook me and reminded me of how vulnerable we are as a Jewish community.

On Rosh Hashanah one of the things we pray for is physical strength in the face of attackers who would like to destroy our people. This message is powerfully conveyed through the symbolism of the shofar.

The first place where the shofar of Rosh Hashanah is mentioned in the Torah is in Vayikra 23:24. The verse states: "The first day of the seventh month shall be a day of rest. It is a *zikhron teruah*, a holy day." The key phrase in this verse is *zikhron teruah*, which literally translates as "a remembrance blast." But that is very difficult to understand – what does it mean to call the sounding of the shofar a remembrance blast? What are we remembering?

Philo of Alexandria, the ancient Jewish theologian, explains that the shofar is a "remembrance blast" in the sense that the shofar was a tool used in the military. The shofar in this sense served different purposes. It was a call to charge, it was a call to retreat, and above all it was a call to remember the ideals and values that the soldiers were fighting for (*De Specialibus Legibus*, trans. F. H. Colson, Loeb Classical Library [1937], 1:180).

In Tanakh, when the shofar was sounded it would most often be associated with the sounds of war. The shofar stands at the center of the greatest military victory in Tanakh – Joshua's defeat of Yericho, which he accomplished simply by blasting the shofar. The shofar stands at the center of the book of Shoftim, when Gidon accomplishes a miraculous victory through the use of the shofar. In short, it is likely that when the people in the time of Tanakh heard the shofar, one of the first thoughts that came to mind was military might.

We are living in a different world today, but the sounds of the shofar connote something similar. Just before we blast the shofar, we read psalm 47. Why psalm 47? Perhaps the psalm is teaching us this connection between the shofar and physical strength. The psalm focuses on the strength of goodness and righteousness in the face of evil.

Verse 2 reads, *"Hariu l'Elokim b'kol rinah."* These words can be translated as a direct command to other false gods: "O false gods of the world, shout out in praise to the true God!" This might also be the way to translate the phrase *"Zamru, elohim, zameru"*: "Sing praises, O false gods, sing praises to Hashem."

No wonder we recite this psalm seven times before we blast the shofar. By doing so we are reenacting Joshua's circling of the walls of Jericho. We are reciting a prayer for physical strength in the face of our enemies. The shofar is a symbol for us to stand strong, to be proud of our values, to have courage in the face of our enemies.

Now more than ever we need that sound of the shofar to resonate purely and to be heard by God. We are living during a time when terrorism seems to be ruling the world in the name of a false theology – a theology which is a distortion of everything true and pure; it is a time when we could easily despair. We need the sound of the shofar – the *zikhron teruah* – to remind us to be strong, to remind us not to waver.

But the same Philo of Alexandria offers another explanation of the phrase *zikhron teruah*. Philo writes that the shofar is intended to be a reminder of the heights that were achieved at Mount Sinai, when the blasts of the shofar rang out from heaven. This approach sees the blasts of the shofar as musical notes that have the ability to teach, to inspire, and to unite. Nowhere were we more united than at Sinai. Nowhere were we educated more effectively than at Sinai. And the sounds that filled our ears at Sinai were the sounds of the shofar.

The sounds of the shofar at Sinai correspond to another symbol of the shofar in the time of Tanakh. Over and over again in Tanakh, the shofar is sounded in order to demonstrate the coronation of a king. When a new king was announced, it was done with the blast of the shofar. This is seen with Avshalom, with Yehu, and with Yoash. The coronation of the king in Tanakh and the coronation of the King of kings at Sinai are both accompanied by the shofar because the shofar is a symbol of unity, of harmony, and of hope.

This understanding of the shofar is also embedded within an alternative reading of psalm 47. We saw before how this psalm could be read as a prophecy of strength in the face of isolation from the evil forces and false gods of the world. A different reading sees it not as a poetic description of physical supremacy, but as a universalistic comment on the reign of God. It's possible to read this psalm as an invitation extended to all the nations of the world to join together in worship of the One God.

According to this approach, verse 2, *"kol haamimim tiku kaf,"* now reads as an invitation to all the nations: Come clap your hands and rejoice in the presence of God. In verses 6 through 8, the psalmist turns to the people who are praying and ushers them along this path: *"Alah Elokim bi'teruah"* (God has gone up with shouting, with the sound of the shofar). Finally, the entire psalm ends with all of the nations of the world coming together to praise God: *"Nedivei amim ne'esafu"* (All of the princes of the world have gathered together in praise of God).

The psalm as a whole now becomes a description of the ascension and coronation of God, King of the universe, upon His heavenly throne. God ascends His throne to the tunes of the shofar and the shouts of the people. The psalm ends with God sitting on His throne with all the nations of the world gathering before Him and recognizing His greatness.

According to this last approach, the reading of psalm 47 immediately before the sounding of the shofar on Rosh Hashanah imitates the heavenly coronation ceremony. As worshippers we are about to perform our own crowning of God. When we sound the shofar, the universal proclamation of dominion, we declare ourselves subservient to the true King of the universe.

In imitation of the shofar blasts at Sinai we sound the shofar. In recognition of God as King we blast the shofar. But according to psalm 47, we do this not out of physical triumphalism, but out of a yearning for universal harmony and recognition of God's mastery. We long for the time when the whole world can gather and, united as one, call out to God.

Perhaps the reason why our tradition selected this psalm as an appropriate reading to precede the shofar blasts is to convey both of these powerful messages. Paradoxically, the sound of the shofar is both a prayer for the physical might and strength of our own people, as well as a prayer for universal harmony in recognizing God's greatness.

How do we understand this paradox? The answer is that we pray for physical strength so that we are able to stand in the face of adversity and proudly teach the values of the Torah – of righteousness, morality, purity – values that we hope will bring harmony and peace to the world.

This double message of the shofar is the prayer that each of us might be making as we hear the blasts of the shofar.

The shofar is a prayer for physical strength so that we can help the world gain peace and harmony. This explains the paradox of psalm 47. This is why the Torah calls Rosh Hashanah *zikhron teruah*, the remembrance of the shofar. For with each blast of the shofar, we remember and pray for both physical security for our people, as well as eternal bliss for the entire world.

Chapter 18
A Modern-Day Meaning to the Akeidah

An acquaintance of mine, Lee, at the American Bible Association, once told me the following story. Lee is a Christian, fully versed in the text of the Bible. It happened that he took his four-year-old son camping. Lee intended to take his son up to a hill so that they could watch the sunrise together and pray. They set out before dawn, and as they reached the dewy grass, Lee's son looked up at him and asked, "Daddy, are we going to Mount Moriah?"

Lee told me that he had never even studied that story with his son. Yet, somehow this little boy had internalized the story of the Akeidah, the story in which God commands Avraham to sacrifice Yitzchak upon Mount Moriah, and only at the very last second does an angel call out to Avraham and say, "Stop!" Lee told me that at that moment, for the first time, he thought to himself, "How could Avraham have gone up that mountain with Yitzchak?"

The Akeidah story pervades the entire *Yamim Noraim*, the period from Rosh Hashanah to Yom Kippur. It is the reading of the second day of Rosh Hashanah, but in fact its story begins on the first day of Rosh Hashanah when we read that Avraham and Sarah are promised a child. It is central to many of the prayers of Rosh Hashanah. We say in Musaf of Rosh Hashanah, "Remember when our father Avraham bound his son Yitzchak on the altar, suppressing his compassion that he might do Your will wholeheartedly." It is central to many of the Selichot that we say during the Days of Awe, and on Yom Kippur itself. We say, "He Who answered Avraham on Mount Moriah, should answer us. He Who answered Yitzchak when he was bound on the altar, should answer us." Finally, the shofar itself, which frames the whole *Yamim Noraim* period, is a reminder of the Akeidah. The shofar comes from a ram, because it reminds us that when Avraham put down Yitzchak, he slaughtered a ram instead. With Avraham's merit we ask to be blessed.

The Akeidah is central to the theme of the Days of Awe. And yet, its message is so difficult ethically. That little boy read the Akeidah story and thought he was next. And maybe he wasn't completely crazy. In 1990, in California, a father – by all accounts a normal, loving, devoted and religious Christian – took his youngest daughter, who was his favorite, and sacrificed her. Can you imagine such a horror! The jury found him insane. But at the trial it came out that he considered himself a modern Avraham.

What message are we trying to send with this ethically difficult story, the Akeidah? Why is its theme central to the *Yamim Noraim*? What can the Akeidah story mean to us when we see the storyline of the Akeidah abused so perversely?

The answer, for me, lies in a midrash that tells of a conversation between Avraham and God. Avraham said to God, "It was only yesterday that You promised me that my seed would go forth from Yitzchak. And now You are telling me, 'Offer him as a sacrifice'?! So too, when Israel will suffer, remember the Akeidah of Yitzchak, and redeem them from their pain" (*Bereishit Rabbah* 56:8; cited by Rashi on Bereishit 22:12).

On a basic level this midrash teaches us that when Israel is in trouble, God will remember the Akeidah, and God will redeem us. However, on a much deeper level, it points to a profound lesson of the Akeidah, and the reason why the Akeidah is so central to the teachings of the Torah.

This midrash is teaching us that the Akeidah is the paradigm of the cycle of life. Avraham is saying to God: "Just yesterday, You told me that I was going to be blessed with a child who would carry my mission forever. And today, you are telling me that my child must die." Just yesterday, Avraham had experienced the greatest joy. And today, God is telling him that he must experience the greatest pain.

And that's the lesson right there. As Freud pointed out, it's a truism of life that the state of happiness can never be maintained forever. Freud said the only way to be truly happy is to remove yourself entirely from the world. Built into all the joy we experience in this world is the understanding that eventually that joy will be turned into sadness. I once sat with a wonderful woman when she learned for the first time that her ninety-year-old husband of sixty years had passed away. She said, "We had such a wonderful life together. Why does this have to happen to me?" She had experienced the greatest joy, and now she was experiencing great pain.

Perhaps God never intended for Avraham to sacrifice Yitzchak. God wished to teach Avraham a fundamental lesson about the patterns of life – both for individuals and as a nation. And so, God used the model of the Akeidah story as a paradigm for life.

The Akeidah teaches us that with all joy comes great pain. And yet, as the midrash says, God will remember the Akeidah and redeem us from that pain. God will not allow us to wallow in our pain forever. In this sense the Akeidah is a story of hope intended to lift us out of our misery, to remind us that God will redeem us from our pain.

The Akeidah promises that joy is followed by pain, which in turn is followed by joy. This theme is actually reflected in the sounds of the shofar itself. In the Torah there are two main terms for the sound of the shofar – the *tekiah* and the *teruah*. Rav Moshe Amiel points out that the Torah refers to the *tekiah* as a blast of joy. The Torah says (Bamidbar 10:10), "On the day of your great rejoicing and on your festivals, you should blast [*u'tekatem*] the trumpets" – the sound of the *tekiah*. On the other hand, the *teruah* – the other sound of the shofar – is associated with trouble and sadness. The Torah instructs us to blow a *teruah* when we go into battle "*al hatzar hatzorer etkhem*" (against the enemy who oppresses you; Bamidbar 10:9). Every shofar blast that we make on Rosh Hashanah is a *tekiah* followed by a *teruah* followed by a *tekiah*. It is the sound of joy followed by the sound of pain, followed by the sound of joy.

On my desk in my office I have a picture of Tomer. I met Tomer on one of my trips to Israel. He is a handsome man, with a successful business, who was wounded in a terrorist attack and is now paralyzed from the waist down. Tomer was devastated. His life had been altered forever. He had been in the hospital bed for months. And yet, when I met him his wife had just given birth to their first child. His pain, as great as it was, began to ebb. He and his wife have the joy of a child. The joy he was feeling at that moment is the joy of the *tekiah gedolah* – the great long *tekiah* blast that follows all the shorter staccato notes of the shofar. I keep Tomer's picture with me on my desk for two reasons: to always have him in mind in my prayers and also to remind myself that no matter how broken a person may be there is always hope that the long blast of the *tekiah* representing our salvation will bring us beyond our sorrows.

Chapter 19
Pray with Power

There is a fairy tale that I remember being told when I was young. There was once a woodcutter who worked tirelessly day and night to provide for his family. One day he came home, exhausted and hungry. Yet he had no food to put on the table.

Suddenly, a fairy came to him and told him, "I will grant you three wishes." Without thinking, the woodcutter said, "I wish I had a sausage." Before he knew it a delicious sausage appeared on the table. When his wife saw this she started screaming at him, "You have three wishes and you wish for a sausage!" He got so upset with her that he said, "I wish that sausage would just stick to your nose." And of course it did. It stuck, and try as they would they could not remove it. The woodcutter had only one wish left. This time he thought long and hard and then said, "I wish that the sausage should come off my wife's nose." He and his wife then enjoyed a sausage for dinner.

This fairy tale can teach us a lot about prayer. We stand on Rosh Hashanah praying for hours and hours. The theme of the day is prayer. We are trying to connect to God and have God answer our prayers. But how can we pray in a way that our prayers are meaningful, in a way that gives us a shot of God answering our prayers? How can we pray without wasting our prayers on the woodcutter's sausage?

The most effective prayer of Rosh Hashanah – perhaps the most effective prayer in all of Jewish history – is the prayer of Chanah (1 Shmuel 1). The Talmud (*Berakhot* 31a) says about Chanah's prayer, "There are many major *halakhot* about prayer that we derive from the prayer of Chanah." This is not said about any other person's prayer in all of Tanakh. It is only Chanah's prayer that stands alone as the paradigm of the way to pray and to connect to God.

What makes Chanah's prayer effective? If you look closely at Chanah's prayer, you can discern seven steps to a great prayer:

1. Prayer from the depths: "*Va'tivkeh v'lo tokhal*" (She cried and did not eat). Year after year Chanah would go up to Shiloh, and year after year she would cry and not eat. She was so down about the fact that she was childless. She was at the bottom. Everyone else was rejoicing and eating – she was crying and unable to eat.

2. Prayer with support: "*Vayomer lah Elkanah, 'Lamah tivki... Halo anokhi tov lakh me'asarah banim'*" (Chanah's husband, Elkanah, said to her, "Why do you cry? ...Am I not better for you than ten sons?"). Chanah was feeling deeply depressed. Yet she was supported by the love of Elkanah. Elkanah reminds her that he loves her deeply.

3. Prayer that affirms life: "*Va'takom Chanah acharei ochlah v'Shiloh v'acharei shatoh*" (And Chanah rose after eating and drinking in Shiloh). Immediately after Chanah hears these words from Elkanah, she participates in the festive

meal. Even if she is still unable to fully rejoice in the meal, she is still there – participating. As a member of the family she rejoices. She partakes in the happy moments of life. She believes in herself. She believes in life.

4. Prayer with courage: *"Va'tomar, 'Hashem Tzevakot'"* (And she said, "Hashem Tzevakot"). Chanah prays with the ultimate courage. In those days, personal, individual prayer was just unheard of. Who prays in the Torah? Only Moshe has the stature to be able to pray to God, to question God. Only the high priest could pray on behalf of all the people. And here comes Chanah. She marches past Eli, the *kohen gadol*. She walks to the center of the sanctuary and she addresses God directly. She calls out, *"Hashem Tzevakot"* (God of Hosts). "Rabbi Elazar said: From the day the Holy One, blessed be He, created the world, no one addressed the Holy One, blessed be He, as Tzevakot until Chanah did" (*Berakhot* 31a). From the day that the world was created, no one had ever had the courage to call out to God and directly address Him the way that Chanah did. Chanah's prayer was courageous because she moved beyond the artificial limits that society and culture had placed on her. She was not afraid of man or God. She was respectful to God, but not afraid of God.

5. Prayer with the proper goals: *"U'netativ l'Hashem kol yemei chayav"* (And I will give him to Hashem all the days of his life). Chanah says to God: "If You grant me a son, then my son will be dedicated to service in the Temple." Chanah asks for a child not so that she can be the equal of her rival, but so that together with her child she can serve God. She asks for a child so that together they can serve the world.

6. Prayer with self-reflection: *"Va'titpallel Chanah"* (And Chanah prayed). The English word "prayer" comes

from the Latin "prector," meaning "beseech." But that is misleading, because that is not what the Hebrew word *tefillah* means. *Tefillah* comes from the word *pillel*, meaning to judge. *Va'titpallel* is cast in the reflexive, meaning that Chanah judged herself. Before Chanah made a request from God she looked within herself. She judged herself. She asked herself how she could improve, how she could grow, how she could speak to God in the proper way. *Va'titpallel Chanah* – Chanah looked within herself, and *then* went to speak to God.

7. Prayer with creativity: "*Sefatehah naot, v'kolah lo yishamea*" (Her lips moved, but her voice was not heard). Chanah was the first person to pray in this self-effacing manner; she was the first person to pray silently. It took enormous creativity and courage to pray in a unique way. Perhaps that's one reason why her prayer was so effective. There is a saying: There is no dance like the first dance. This means that the first person who danced did so with such creativity, spontaneity, warmth, and love, that no other dance was ever able to equal the fervor and the passion of that dance. Chanah's prayer was said with such tenderness, uniqueness, and love that no prayer has ever been able to approach it.

These are the basic tools of prayer. We all need to pray. We need to pray on both a national level and on a personal level.

That's where we should begin our prayers. Begin with our greatest challenges, our greatest struggles. Begin from the depths. Think about what our real problems are and then begin to pray.

The next step is to pray with support. It is not an accident that our rabbis told us to pray in a minyan. By praying together we create a community, we create a family. When we pray together we surround ourselves with the love and support of a community.

Pray by affirming life. Pray with the belief that anything can happen. Pray with the belief that God can perform miracles. Pray with the belief that there is the possibility that it will be OK. Pray by believing in yourself and believing in life.

Pray with courage. We can't sell ourselves short. Let's not settle for anything from God or from life. This is what it means to pray with courage. Ask God to help us fulfill our deepest dreams. Chanah prayed with chutzpah and utter honesty – and so should we. What do we *really* want the most? Don't be afraid or ashamed to tell God what that is.

Pray with the proper goals. Chanah promises that she will raise the child for God's sake. Prayer is not just "Gimme," but "Give me so that I can contribute to Your world." Once Chanah started thinking in those terms, she began to appreciate how many blessings she had in this world and how much she could give to others. If she had not had a child, she might have found another way to be of service. Prayer should change our perspective from what we need to what we can give.

Pray with self-reflection. Prayer is the time to look within and to assess our lives. Are we going where we want to? Are we really asking for what we need? When we pray with self-reflection, then we will also be praying with the proper goals.

A story is told by the Rebbe of Roptchitz. During the siege of Sebastopol Czar Nicholas was once riding along the walls when an enemy archer tried to shoot him. A Russian soldier who saw this, screamed, which alerted the Czar and saved his life. The Czar told the man to ask any favor that he wanted. "Our sergeant is so harsh," cried he soldier. "He is always beating me. If only I could serve a different sergeant!" "Fool," cried Nicholas, "be a sergeant yourself!" (Martin Buber, *Tales of the Hasidim*, "The Later Masters," 194).

Let's not make that same mistake. Let's pray with our deepest dreams and deepest desires. Let's believe in the power of prayer.

Most of all, let's pray with great creativity. Pray with romance. Let's lose ourselves in the warmth of the prayer. Let's try to connect to God in a way that we have never connected before.

When Rabbi Moshe Leib of Sassov needed to pray for a situation of great need he first put on new shoes made of the finest leather. He then laced them tightly, and danced. A tzaddik who once witnessed this type of intense preparation for prayer and the powerful dance that accompanied the prayer said: "Power flowed forth from the dancing. Every step was a mystery. A new light suffused the house, and everyone watching saw the heavenly hosts join in his dance" (Buber, ibid., 90).

Chapter 20
True, Honest Jews

The story of the Akeidah is familiar. God commands Avraham to sacrifice his only son Yitzchak. But how could Avraham do it? How could he take his son to the altar and sacrifice him?

Rambam explains in the *Guide to the Perplexed* that the very fact that Avraham was willing to take his son to the altar proves that Avraham had received this prophecy from God with absolute certainty and clarity. If Avraham was not absolutely sure what God was telling him, then there is no way he would have been willing to sacrifice his son. As Rambam writes, "If a prophecy was not completely clear then no prophet would be willing to do that which was unnatural. Avraham would never have agreed to offer his son as an offering unless he was absolutely certain that God had spoken to him" (*Guide* 3:24).

Rambam is arguing that Avraham was only able to perform this act because he heard a clear, unambiguous commandment from God. Only someone who has heard the word of God directly could prepare themselves to perform the unthinkable act that Avraham was about to do.

The great Izbica Rebbe is bothered by Rambam's approach. Asks the Izbica, if Rambam is correct, then what was the big deal about what Avraham did? Can you imagine anyone not listening to the word of God? If God says something to you, then of course you have to do it.

So the Izbica offers a new interpretation of the Akeidah. The challenge of the Akeidah was not that Avraham had to force himself to obey the clear teaching of God, *but that he had to obey God even though God's teaching was not clear.*

> The fundamental challenge of the Akeidah was that Avraham had already received one explicit teaching from God – "Thou shall not kill" – and certainly not his own son. (Izbicer Rebbe, *Mei Hashiloach*, parashat Vayera)

Yet, now Avraham was hearing another teaching – a second, contradictory teaching. The voice of God was telling him to kill his own son. The Izbica writes that Avraham was confused; he could have justified himself by deciding this dilemma in either direction. It wasn't crystal clear what God was saying to him. But deep down he really knew what God wanted – and that was the challenge.

The challenge of the Akeidah was for Avraham to be true to himself. He could have found a way to justify whatever he did. He had different ways to rationalize his behavior. Yet deep down he knew which commandment of God was clearer, which commandment needed to observed. The whole challenge of the Akeidah was: Would Avraham be honest with himself?

This is the question that we should be asking ourselves on Rosh Hashanah. Do we know who we are? Do we know what we believe in? Do we know what our goals are? Are we being honest with ourselves?

One time I traveled with Rabbi Avi Weiss and spent Shabbat at the University of Michigan in support of Israel. It was a difficult Shabbat because we were there in solidarity with Israel but there was also an opposition group present that was encouraging the university to stop investing in Israel. The campus was polarized, with many students supporting Israel and others attacking it. It was a tough time for a lot of the Jewish students on campus. They were being asked to make difficult decisions about who they were and what they believed in.

We spent Friday night talking to a group of students in the Chabad house. We had a wonderful evening connecting with the actively involved students on the campus. But then we decided to go for a walk on the campus. We walked down fraternity row, and somehow we struck up a conversation with a Jewish kid who had thus far spent his Friday nights partying with his fraternity. This boy had never been to Hebrew school, and he told us that he never went to the Hillel. But he got really excited when he heard that we were rabbis. His whole face lit up and he started talking to us seriously. Then his friends came over and said, "Come on, man, let's go to the party." And he said, "No, you guys don't understand, I'm talking to rabbis. I'm Jewish. This is incredible."

In that moment, that student knew who he was. He didn't want to go the party. He wanted to talk to us because he realized he was Jewish.

That's what these Days of Awe are all about. They are about reminding us that we can't run away from ourselves. We can't deny our true selves.

The very last passage that we read on Yom Kippur is the reading from the prophet Yonah. God says to Yonah, "*Kum! Lekh el Nineveh*" (Get up! Go to Nineveh). Fulfill your mission. Go and prophesize.

Yonah tries to run, to escape God. "*Va'yakam Yonah livroach*" – Yonah arises, not to fulfill his mission, but to flee – to run away from God. But of course, we know that that is an impossibility.

This theme is reinforced through a prayer that dominates Rosh Hashanah – the Aleinu prayer. Aleinu was a prayer originally composed to be read before the shofar blowing. It is a prayer that appears in the Musaf Amidah on both days of Rosh Hashanah. In Aleinu we declare, *"she'lo asanu k'goyei haaratzot...she'lo sam chelkenu kahem v'goralenu k'khol hamonam"* – You did not make us like all the other nations. We are unique. We have our own lot on this earth. *"Va'anachnu korim u'mishtachavim u'modim"* – Our mission is simple. It is to call out to the world about the greatness of God and the greatness of His world. It is to spread the light about God in the world. Our mission is to recognize that God is calling each of us. It is to be true to ourselves, to allow ourselves to fulfill our roles before God.

There was once a great rebbe named Reb Shlomo Chayyim of Kaidanov. Before he died, he gathered his children around him and said, "Don't think of your father as a tzaddik or a rebbe. But at the same time, I wasn't a hypocrite. I tried to live my life as a Jew."

It is a worthy goal to simply try to live our life as true, honest Jews.

Chapter 21
Let Us Listen

The Torah reading for the first day of Rosh Hashanah is very much about the power of listening.

The reading tells us the story of Yitzchak and Yishmael. Sarah and Avraham had been married for many years without a child, when Sarah directed Avraham to have a child with her servant, Hagar. Hagar gives birth to Yishmael. But then God remembers Sarah and she too has a child, Yitzchak. Sarah does not like the way Yishmael is interacting with Yitzchak and so she expels Yishmael from her house. Yishmael is sent out from the home to protect Yitzchak.

As Jews, the biological descendants of Yitzchak, we often read this story from his point of view. Sarah protects Yitzchak. She makes sure that there is no barrier in his path to inheriting the legacy of Avraham. As Jews we are thankful that Yitzchak wins out.

But let's also look at the story from Yishmael's perspective. Here is a child who for thirteen years was viewed as the prince. He was the child who would carry on the great work of Avraham. Suddenly a new child is born and not only will he not inherit from his father, but he is expelled – cast out in the desert, with only his mother to protect him.

What did Yishmael actually do to deserve this punishment? The verse states, "Sarah saw the son of Hagar the Egyptian laughing [*metzachek*]. And she said to Avraham, 'Drive out this slave woman with her son'" (Bereishit 21:9–10). According to the straightforward meaning, Sarah kicked Yishmael out because he was laughing. It doesn't seem fair. The rabbis struggle with the literal words of the text. They can't fathom that Yishmael didn't do anything wrong, so they ascribe to him terrible sins.

Rashi, quoting the Midrash (*Bereishit Rabbah* 53:11), says that Yishmael committed the sins of idolatry, murder, and licentiousness – the worst three crimes in the Jewish religion. The very fact that Rashi is moved to such extreme language hints to the possibility that he is overcompensating in justifying how an innocent person could be expelled. Rashi's answer is that Yishmael must not have been innocent.

But we have a concept in Judaism, "*Ein mikra yotzei midei peshuto.*" We can never forget the literal words of the text. And, literally, all Yishmael did was laugh. He laughed and for this he was thrown out of his own home. He was picked on for no reason.

How many of us feel beaten up by life? How many of us feel that we got a rough deal from God? When I think of people who got a rough deal from God, I think of my friends Joe and Goldie. Joe and Goldie are Holocaust survivors. They each spent time in the horrible concentration camps. They each lost many family members in the Shoah. But they came here to America and built a life. They had a child, Henry, who was so talented in every area of life but tragically succumbed to cancer before he could marry and begin his own family.

I remember sitting in the room as Henry died, watching my friends Joe and Goldie. Here were people who had gotten a raw deal from God. They never asked for much; all they really wanted was for their child to outlive them.

In this sense, their voice can be heard through the voice of Yishmael. He is the voice of people who feel rejected by God.

In the words of one commentator on the Torah, "Ishmael is the voice of the outcast, the orphan, the part of our community that has been uprooted, branded...or made into the enemy" (Peter Pitzele, *Our Fathers' Wells: A Personal Encounter with the Myths of Genesis* [HarperCollins, 1996], 115). As Jews, we are biologically descendants of Yitzchak. But as people, it often feels as though we are the descendants of Yishmael. On different levels, we have all been rejected, scorned, made to feel unwelcome by God. We all have had hardships in life. For some, they have been minor, for others, massive. But we all have had challenges.

Maybe this is why we read this story on Rosh Hashanah. No matter the goodness and the grace that God shines down upon us, many of us only feel rejected by Him. We feel that we have no place in God's canopy, that we are not welcome. We feel that we are not the chosen ones. We feel unloved by God.

Rosh Hashanah reminds us that despite everything we are all loved by God. It might not always seem that way, but God promises us that He does love us. On Rosh Hashanah, God is crowned King, King of the universe, Who created all creatures. But even more than He is King of the universe, He is *Avinu Malkeinu*, the King Who is our parent, a loving parent Who always embraces us.

At the beginning of the story, Yishmael is not called by name; he is referred to only as *"ben Hagar haMitzrit"* (the son of Hagar the Egyptian woman). It is as though he is unimportant; he has no name, and no one will listen to him.

But God hears him. The name Yishmael means "God will hear." God promises that He will hear the voices of the rejected, the unloved. Yishmael was thrown out into the desert. His water disappeared, but God heard him. "God heard the voice of the boy" – the voice no one wanted to hear, God heard. And an angel of God called out to Hagar from heaven and declared, "Have no fear, for God has heard the voice of the lad."

In the end, God will hear.

This is the welcoming embrace of Rosh Hashanah. Too many of us feel that God does not love us, that life is unfair. We are all Yishmael. But God reaches out and tells us He loves us. God will hear our prayers. God will listen to us.

In the haftarah for the first day we read about Chanah. She came childless to the Temple seeking to pour out her heart to God. But the high priest, Eli, didn't trust her. He thought she was drunk. No one listened to her voice, and when she prayed she spoke so softly that no one could hear – no one except God. That's why Chanah names her son Shmuel, meaning, *shamah El* (God heard). Chanah had been rejected; she had felt insignificant and empty. But in the end God heard her voice and embraced her.

Being loved by God is not only a sweet, welcoming thought. It is also a challenge. It may be the central command of Rosh Hashanah. On Rosh Hashanah we remind ourselves that it is our responsibility to emulate God, to be as much as possible like God. It is our responsibility to hear the voices of the rejected, to listen to the scorned, and to hear the cries of people who don't know how to speak.

This is a fundamental message of the shofar. It is the purest prayer, the prayer without words. It is the cry of people who can't formulate their words, the cry of people who feel rejected.

As religious communities we welcome these people into our congregations on Rosh Hashanah. More than that, we place their cries at the center of our prayers. We remind ourselves that God has commanded us not to blast the shofar – *litkoa kol shofar* – but "*lishmoa kol shofar*," to hear the cries of the shofar, to hear the cries of the rejected.

Today we hear more about religions rejecting people than about religions accepting and loving people. For me the purpose of religion is less to preach against the immoral vices of the world, and more to remind us of our responsibility to the Yishmaels of the world. Especially in a synagogue, our job is to hear the voice. My primary responsibility as rabbi is not to teach, but really to listen – to listen to the voices of the congregation, to listen to the cries of people.

Rosh Hashanah reminds us that God will always love us. He will always embrace us. He will hear our prayers. But at the same time we must follow the ways of God. We must listen to everyone in our communities. Our synagogues must be places where all are made to feel welcome, where no one is excluded. Our synagogues must be extra-sensitive to the needs of the elderly, the physically challenged, the mentally challenged, the religious novices, lonely people, unsuccessful people, people who have suffered.

This is the commandment of listening to the shofar on Rosh Hashanah. It's a reminder: As God listens to us, we must listen to others.